Introduction to the Gospel of Matthew

Introduction to the Gospel of Matthew

under the supervision of
William H. Malas Jr

Theological Essentials

DTL

Library of Congress Cataloging-in-Publication Data

William H. Malas Jr (creator).
Introduction to the Gospel of Matthew / William H. Malas Jr

134 + xiv pp. cm. 12.7 x 20.32
ISBN 979-8-89731-389-1 (Print)
ISBN 979-8-89731-257-3 (Ebook)
ISBN 979-8-89731-262-7 (Kindle)
ISBN 979-8-89731-268-9 (Abridged Audio Discussion)
     1. Bible. Matthew — Introductions.
     2. Bible. Matthew — Criticism, interpretation, etc.
BS2580 .M35 2026

This book is available as an Open Access book in multiple languages at www.DTLPress.com

Cover Image: "Rest on the Flight into Egypt," by Donal Hord
Photo Credit: DTL Staff.

Contents

Series Preface

Artificial Intelligence (AI) is changing everything, including theological scholarship and education. This series, *Theological Essentials*, is designed to bring the creative potential of AI to the field of theological education. In the traditional model, a scholar with both mastery of the scholarly discourse and a record of successful classroom teaching would spend several months — or even several years — writing, revising and rewriting an introductory text which would then be transferred to a publisher who also invested months or years in production processes. Even though the end product was typically quite predictable, this slow and expensive process caused the prices of textbooks to balloon. As a result, students in developed nations paid more than they should have for the books and students in developing nations typically had no access to these (cost-prohibitive) textbooks until they appeared as discards and donations decades later. In previous generations, the need for quality assurance — in the form of content generation, expert review, copy-editing and printing time — may have made this slow, expensive and exclusionary approach inevitable. However, AI is changing everything.

This series is very different; it is created by AI. The cover of each volume identifies the work as "created under the supervision of" an expert in the field. However, that person is not an author in the traditional sense. The creator of each volume has been trained by the DTL staff in the use of AI and *the creator has used AI to create, edit, revise and recreate the text that you see*. With that creation process clearly identified, let me explain the goals of this series.

Our Goals

Credibility: Although AI has made — and continues to make — huge strides over the last few years, no unsupervised AI can create a truly reliable or fully credible college or seminary level text. The limitations of AI generated content sometimes originates from the limitations of the content itself (the training set may be inadequate), but more often, user dissatisfaction with AI-generated content arises from human errors associated with poor prompt engineering. The DTL Press has sought to overcome both of these problems by hiring established scholars with widely recognized expertise to create books within their areas of expertise and by training those scholars and experts in AI prompt engineering. To be clear, the scholar whose name appears on the cover of this work has created this volume — generating, reading, regenerating, rereading and revising the work. Even though the work was generated (in varying degrees) by AI, the names of our scholarly creators appear on the cover as a guarantee that the content is equally credible with any introductory work which that scholar/creator would pen using the traditional model.

Stability: AI is generative, meaning that the response to each prompt is uniquely generated for that specific request. No two AI-generated responses are precisely the same. The inevitable variability of AI responses presents a significant pedagogical challenge for professors and students who wish to begin their discussions and analysis on the basis of a shared set of ideas. Educational institutions need stable texts in order to prevent pedagogical chaos. These books provide that stable text from which to teach, discuss and engage ideas.

Affordability: The DTL Press is committed to the idea that affordability should not be a barrier to knowledge. *All persons are equally deserving of the right to know and to understand.* Therefore, ebook versions of all DTL Press books are available from the DTL libraries without charge, and available as print books for a nominal fee. Our scholar/creators are to be thanked for their willingness to forego traditional royalty arrangements. (Our creators are compensated for their generative work, but they do not receive royalties in the traditional sense.)

Accessibility: The DTL Press would like to make high quality, low cost introductory textbooks available to everyone, everywhere in the world. The books in this series are immediately made available in multiple languages. The DTL Press will create translations in other languages upon request. Translations are, of course, generated by AI.

Our Acknowledged Limitations

Some readers are undoubtedly thinking, "but AI can only produce derivative scholarship;

AI can't create original, innovative scholarship." That criticism is, of course, largely accurate. AI is largely limited to aggregating, organizing and repackaging pre-existing ideas (although sometimes in ways that can be used to accelerate and refine the production of original scholarship). Still while acknowledging this inherent limitation of AI, the DTL Press would offer two comments: (1) Introductory texts are seldom meant to be truly ground breaking in their originality and (2) the DTL Press has other series dedicated to publishing original scholarship with traditional authorship.

Our Invitation

The DTL Press would like to fundamentally reshape academic publishing in the theological world to make scholarship more accessible and more affordable in two ways. First, we would like to generate introductory texts in all areas of theological discourse, so that no one is ever forced to "buy a textbook" in any language. It is our vision for professors anywhere to be able to use one book, two books or an entire set of books in this series as the *introductory* textbooks for their classes. Second, we would also like to publish traditionally authored scholarly monographs for Open Access (free) distribution for an advanced scholarly readership.

Finally, the DTL Press is non-confessional and will publish works in any area of religious studies. Traditionally authored books are peer-reviewed; AI-generated introductory book creation is open to anyone with the required expertise to supervise content generation in that area of discourse. If you share the DTL Press's commitment to credibility, affordability and accessibility, contact us about changing the world of theological publishing by contributing to this series or a more traditionally authored series.

With high expectations,
Thomas E. Phillips
DTL Press Executive Director
www.thedtl.org
www.DTLpress.com

Part I
Foundations and Frameworks

Chapter 1
Introduction to Matthean Studies

The Gospel of Matthew occupies a distinctive place within the New Testament canon and the history of Christian interpretation. Although traditionally listed first among the four canonical Gospels, Matthew is not chronologically the earliest. The position it holds at the head of the New Testament reflects both its early and sustained importance in the life of the church and its role as a bridge between the Hebrew Scriptures and the story of Jesus Christ. From its opening genealogy, which anchors Jesus within Israel's sacred history, to its climactic commission to "make disciples of all nations" (28:19), Matthew presents a narrative that is at once deeply Jewish and profoundly universal. For this reason, the Gospel has long been regarded as a foundational text for Christian identity, theology, and practice.

The Place of Matthew in the Canon

The placement of Matthew at the beginning of the New Testament canon was not accidental. Its seamless integration of Old Testament quotations and fulfillment motifs made it appear as a natural continuation of Israel's Scriptures. Patristic writers frequently emphasized Matthew's role as a "gateway" into the Christian story. Irenaeus, for example, described it as the first written Gospel and identified it as particularly suited for Jewish believers. Although modern scholarship disputes Irenaeus's historical claims, the canonical ordering of the Gospels reflects the longstanding perception that Matthew's narrative best serves as an introduction to the person and mission of Jesus.

A Survey of Matthean Scholarship

The interpretation of Matthew has undergone significant shifts across the centuries. Early patristic interpreters read Matthew in harmony with the other Gospels, often highlighting its teaching on ecclesial order and moral instruction. Medieval commentators, such as Thomas Aquinas, mined Matthew for theological synthesis and ethical application. The Reformation era renewed attention to Matthew's emphasis on law and righteousness, leading to varied interpretations among Protestant reformers concerning the Sermon on the Mount and the relationship between law and gospel.

The rise of modern biblical criticism introduced new methods and fresh questions. In the nineteenth century, scholars placed Matthew at the center of debates over the "Synoptic Problem," examining its literary relationship to Mark and Luke. Twentieth-century research focused increasingly on Matthew's distinctive redactional tendencies, identifying how the evangelist reshaped his sources to articulate particular theological convictions. More recently, narrative and literary-critical approaches have highlighted the Gospel's plot, characterization, and symbolic motifs, while theological and canonical readings have re-emphasized its role within the broader witness of Scripture.

Hermeneutical Approaches

No single interpretive method suffices to capture the complexity of Matthew's Gospel. Historical-critical tools remain essential for reconstructing the Gospel's *Sitz im Leben*, or "life setting," in the context of first-century Judaism and early Christianity. These include analysis of sources, traditions, and redactional strategies. At the same time, literary approaches shed light on Matthew's artistry, such as his structuring of Jesus' teachings into five major discourses or his use of typology to present Jesus as a new Moses.

Theological interpretation, both ancient and modern, insists that Matthew must be read not merely as a historical artifact but as a witness to divine revelation. Reception history reminds us that the Gospel's meaning has always been shaped within the communities that read and proclaimed it from early church fathers to contemporary theologians across diverse global contexts. For seminary students and scholars alike, a fruitful approach to Matthew is therefore integrative: it engages critically with historical and literary questions while also attending to the Gospel's ongoing theological and ecclesial significance.

The Task Ahead

This textbook aims to equip students with the tools necessary to interpret Matthew responsibly and rigorously. Such study requires careful attention to historical context, sensitivity to literary form, and openness to theological insight. As the opening section of the New Testament canon, Matthew introduces us not only to the story of Jesus but also to the very challenges and opportunities inherent in the task of Gospel interpretation.

Chapter 2
Authorship, Date, and Provenance

Questions of authorship, dating, and provenance are foundational for understanding the Gospel of Matthew. While these issues cannot be answered with absolute certainty, they provide critical context for situating the Gospel historically and theologically. The exploration of these questions also reveals the interplay between early Christian tradition and modern critical scholarship, each contributing important insights for interpretation.

Authorship

The traditional ascription of the Gospel to the apostle Matthew, also known as Levi the tax collector, goes back to the second century. Early church writers such as Papias, Irenaeus, and Origen identified Matthew as the author, often emphasizing that he composed his account initially for Jewish Christians. This attribution gave the Gospel significant authority in the patristic period, aligning it with one of the Twelve who had followed Jesus directly.

Modern scholarship, however, raises doubts about apostolic authorship. Several considerations make it unlikely that the historical Matthew wrote the Gospel in its present form. First, the Gospel is heavily dependent on the Gospel of Mark, which would be unusual if an eyewitness were writing independently. Second, the work is composed in polished Greek and reflects sophisticated literary structure, which suggests composition by a skilled author trained in the conventions of Greco-Roman writing. Third, the Gospel seems to presuppose a community already wrestling with the separation from the synagogue, a situation more characteristic of a post-apostolic context. For these reasons, most contemporary scholars regard the author as an anonymous Jewish-Christian teacher or scribe who was deeply rooted in Israel's Scriptures and traditions.

Date

The dating of Matthew is closely connected to questions of authorship and context. Traditional church history sometimes placed it early, even in the 50s or 60s CE, though this view has little support today. More commonly, scholars situate the Gospel in the last quarter of the first century.

A majority view places Matthew in the 80s or early 90s CE, after the destruction of the Jerusalem Temple in 70 CE. This is suggested by several factors: Matthew's heightened concern with the relationship between Israel and the church, its attention to the ongoing role of the law, and its retrospective tone regarding the mission to Israel and the nations. Certain passages, such as the parable of the wedding banquet in Matthew 22, may reflect knowledge of the destruction of Jerusalem, casting it as divine judgment.

A minority of scholars argue for a pre-70 date, suggesting that Matthew's portrayal of the Temple and its institutions could fit a still-functioning cultic context. However, the balance of evidence points to a post-70 setting, where the traumatic loss of the Temple and the reshaping of Jewish identity provide the backdrop for Matthew's portrayal of Jesus as the fulfillment of Israel's story.

Provenance

The complex and debated question of provenance focuses on the location where Matthew was written and the community it addressed. Early church tradition often associated Matthew with a Jewish-Christian community in Palestine. While possible, internal evidence in the Gospel points to a more diverse and Hellenistic setting.

Many scholars favor Antioch in Syria as the most likely place of origin. Antioch was a major urban center with a significant Jewish population and one of the earliest centers of Christian activity. It was also a context where disputes between Jews and Christians, and within Christian groups themselves, were particularly intense. Matthew's strong concern with Jewish law, synagogue conflict, and mission to the Gentiles resonates with the kinds of tensions likely present in Antioch.

Other proposals include Galilee, due to Matthew's geographical focus, and Alexandria, given its strong Jewish community and history of interpretive traditions. Ultimately, no single location can be established with certainty, but the

Gospel clearly reflects a community negotiating its identity in the aftermath of the destruction of the Temple and in the midst of conflict with emerging rabbinic Judaism.

Conclusion

While the Gospel of Matthew cannot be securely tied to the apostle Matthew, its traditional attribution highlights the deep connections early Christians saw between this text and the apostolic witness. Modern scholarship more cautiously situates the Gospel in the late first century, likely in a mixed Jewish-Christian community in Syria or another major center of early Christianity. Recognizing the Gospel's post-70 context helps modern interpreters appreciate its urgent concerns: defining continuity with Israel's Scriptures, grappling with the meaning of the law, and proclaiming the universal mission of Jesus the Messiah.

Chapter 3
Sources and Composition

The Gospel of Matthew, like the other Synoptics, did not emerge in a vacuum. Understanding its sources and composition is critical for interpreting its distinctive features and theological aims. Modern study of Matthew has been deeply shaped by the Synoptic Problem, the question of how Matthew, Mark, and Luke are literarily related. Consideration of sources, oral tradition, and redaction illuminates both the Gospel's dependence on earlier materials and its creative shaping of them.

The Synoptic Problem

The similarities among Matthew, Mark, and Luke are too striking to be explained by coincidence. At the same time, their differences point to deliberate authorial choices. The prevailing solution in modern scholarship is the Two-Source Hypothesis, which proposes that both Matthew and Luke used Mark as a primary source, while also drawing upon a second source, often referred to as Q (from the German *Quelle*, meaning "source"). Q is understood as a hypothetical collection of Jesus' sayings, reconstructed on the basis of material common to Matthew and Luke but absent from Mark, such as the Lord's Prayer and the Beatitudes.

Alternative hypotheses exist. The Farrer Hypothesis argues that Luke used both Mark and Matthew, thereby eliminating the need for Q. The Griesbach Hypothesis (or Two-Gospel Hypothesis) suggests that Matthew was written first, Luke second, and Mark as a condensed version of both. Despite ongoing debate, the majority of scholars still regard the Two-Source Hypothesis as the most plausible explanation, given the extensive verbal agreement between Matthew and Mark and the difficulty of explaining Matthew's dependence on Luke.

Matthew's Use of Mark

If Matthew indeed used Mark as a source, he did not simply reproduce it mechanically. Careful comparison shows that Matthew reshaped Mark in ways that reveal his theological and pastoral priorities. For instance, Matthew tends to abbreviate Mark's narratives, smoothing out rough details and heightening literary polish. He often strengthens Christological titles, referring to Jesus as "Lord" where Mark calls him "Teacher." Matthew also expands on Mark's teaching material, inserting additional sayings that align with his concern for discipleship and ethical instruction.

These editorial moves show that Matthew was not merely a compiler but a purposeful theologian. His use of Mark reveals both continuity with earlier tradition and the interpretive freedom to present Jesus' story in ways most meaningful for his community.

The Role of Q and Other Traditions

If Q or similar collections of Jesus' sayings were available to Matthew, they would have supplied much of the teaching material that is characteristic of his Gospel. The Sermon on the Mount, for example, contains large blocks of material that scholars assign to this source. Whether Q was a written document or an oral tradition remains debated, but Matthew's integration of such sayings into carefully structured discourses demonstrates his skill in shaping tradition for theological ends.

Beyond Mark and Q, Matthew likely drew upon special sources unique to his Gospel, often labeled M material. These include the infancy narratives (chapters 1–2), certain parables such as the parable of the weeds (13:24–30), and unique narrative details in the passion and resurrection accounts. These traditions may have circulated orally within Matthew's community or been preserved in smaller written collections.

Redaction and Composition

The study of Matthew's distinctive shaping of sources (i.e., his redaction of them) provides valuable insight into his theological agenda. By arranging Jesus' teachings into five major discourses, Matthew highlights the image of Jesus as a new Moses, delivering instruction that both fulfills and transcends the Torah. By introducing formula quotations such as "This was to fulfill what was spoken by the prophet...," Matthew emphasizes the continuity of Jesus' ministry with

Israel's Scriptures. By giving prominence to Peter and the disciples, Matthew underscores the authority and mission of the church.

The composition of Matthew thus represents a dynamic interplay of tradition and innovation. The evangelist worked with inherited material but reorganized and reinterpreted it in light of his community's needs and his theological convictions. The result is a Gospel that is both firmly rooted in the earliest Jesus tradition and creatively adapted to address the challenges of a post-70 Jewish-Christian setting.

Conclusion

Matthew's Gospel reflects a complex process of composition, drawing on Mark, shared traditions, and unique sources. The evangelist's careful redaction demonstrates his role not only as a transmitter of tradition but as a theological author in his own right. Recognizing the ways Matthew reshaped his sources helps interpreters appreciate the distinctive voice of the first Gospel and its enduring theological contribution.

Chapter 4
Historical and Cultural Context

Any responsible interpretation of Matthew must take seriously the historical and cultural world in which it was composed. The Gospel did not emerge in isolation but reflects the social, religious, and political realities of the first-century Mediterranean world. Attending to this background helps modern readers understand both the continuities between Matthew's message and Jewish tradition, as well as the tensions that arose between Matthew's community and its surrounding environment.

Judaism in the First Century

Matthew's Gospel is deeply embedded in the life and thought of Second Temple Judaism. The opening genealogy, the frequent citation of Israel's Scriptures, and the sustained attention to the law all testify to a writer and community steeped in Jewish tradition. Yet the Judaism of Matthew's time was not monolithic. The first century witnessed a rich diversity of Jewish movements and interpretations of Torah, which included the priestly leadership of the Sadducees, the legal precision of the Pharisees, the separatist piety of the Essenes, and the revolutionary zeal of other groups.

The destruction of the Temple in 70 CE radically altered this landscape. With the priestly system dismantled, authority shifted increasingly to the Pharisaic and rabbinic traditions, which emphasized Torah study, synagogue worship, and community discipline as the means of preserving Jewish identity. It is against this backdrop that Matthew presents Jesus as the fulfillment of Israel's story, one who both upholds and redefines Torah in ways that often brought his followers into conflict with synagogue authorities.

The Roman Imperial Setting

Equally important for understanding Matthew is the broader Greco-Roman context. The eastern provinces of the Roman Empire were marked by imperial control, economic exploitation, and cultural pluralism. Roman governors, soldiers, and tax collectors were constant reminders of foreign domination. Although Matthew rarely refers explicitly to Rome, the realities of empire form the unspoken background to many of the Gospel's themes. Jesus' proclamation of the "kingdom of heaven" offered a counter-claim to imperial power, suggesting that true authority lies not in Caesar but in God's reign.

At the same time, Matthew reflects the complexities of living under empire. The command to "render to Caesar the things that are Caesar's, and to God the things that are God's" (22:21) illustrates the negotiation required of a community navigating loyalty to God while living under Roman rule. The Gospel's emphasis on persecution and endurance also resonates with the experiences of believers whose allegiance to Jesus placed them at odds with both civic and religious authorities.

The World of Early Christianity
Matthew also reflects the internal dynamics of early Christian communities. By the time of its composition, the Jesus movement had spread beyond its Palestinian origins into urban centers of the Mediterranean world. Communities were composed of both Jewish and Gentile believers, which created tensions over issues such as observance of the law, table fellowship, and identity markers like circumcision and Sabbath.

Matthew's Gospel addresses precisely these questions. On the one hand, it insists on continuity with Israel, presenting Jesus as the one who fulfills the law and the prophets. On the other hand, it highlights the mission to the nations, culminating in the Great Commission to make disciples of all peoples. This dual concern suggests that Matthew's community was itself negotiating how to remain faithful to its Jewish heritage while embracing the universal scope of the gospel.

Conclusion
The historical and cultural context of Matthew is marked by three overlapping realities: the diversity and transformation of first-century Judaism, the pervasive influence of Roman imperial power, and the expanding reach of early Christianity. Understanding these forces provides essential background for interpreting Matthew's Gospel. It reveals the evangelist as a theologian

who addressed the urgent questions of identity, faithfulness, and mission in a time of profound transition.

Part II
Literary Shape and Structure

Chapter 5
Genre and Narrative Dynamics

The Gospel of Matthew, like the other canonical Gospels, presents itself as a narrative account of the life, teachings, death, and resurrection of Jesus. Yet questions of genre and literary form are crucial for interpretation. Understanding Matthew as a work of ancient literature situates it within the conventions of its time, while attention to its narrative dynamics sheds light on how the Gospel communicates meaning through plot, character, and symbolism.

The Gospel as Ancient Biography

Modern scholarship generally classifies the canonical Gospels as examples of Greco-Roman biography (*bios*). Ancient biographies were not exhaustive life histories in the modern sense, but selective portrayals intended to illuminate the character, significance, and exemplary actions of their subject. Matthew shares key features with this genre: it focuses on a single individual, it structures events to highlight the subject's identity and mission, and it integrates sayings and deeds as expressions of character.

At the same time, Matthew departs from typical *bioi* in significant ways. The narrative is framed not merely as a record of Jesus' greatness but as an announcement of God's saving action in history. The inclusion of miraculous events, fulfillment of prophecy, and the climactic resurrection pushes the Gospel beyond conventional biography into the realm of theological narrative. Matthew is therefore both like and unlike other works of its literary environment. Thus, Matthew is similar enough to be recognized as a biography, but distinctive in its theological aim.

Narrative Strategies

Matthew employs deliberate narrative strategies to shape the story of Jesus. The Gospel is carefully structured, beginning with an infancy narrative that situates Jesus within Israel's history, moving through a ministry in Galilee, climaxing in the passion at Jerusalem, and concluding with resurrection and commission. This narrative arc guides the reader from promise to fulfillment, from revelation to mission.

Characterization is central to Matthew's narrative technique. Jesus is consistently portrayed as authoritative in word and deed, often in contrast to opponents such as the Pharisees and scribes. The disciples are presented with complexity. At times they are exemplary in their response, yet they are also prone to misunderstanding and failure. This dual portrayal underscores both the call to faithful discipleship and the reality of human weakness. Secondary figures, including crowds, women, Gentiles, and even Roman officials, play important roles in demonstrating the breadth of Jesus' impact. For example, the Canaanite woman's persistent faith (15:21–28) and the centurion's recognition of

Jesus' authority (8:5–13) both anticipate the inclusion of the nations. Likewise, Pilate's wife (27:19) functions as an unexpected witness, and the women at the tomb (28:1–10) emerge as the first heralds of the resurrection.

Matthew also uses symbolic settings to shape meaning. Galilee serves as the place of revelation and teaching, Jerusalem as the locus of conflict and rejection. Mountains are frequent sites of teaching and revelation, evoking Sinai and underscoring Jesus' role as a new Moses. The interplay of geography and narrative function reflects Matthew's literary artistry.

Themes of Plot and Movement

The Gospel's plot is not simply a chronological record but a theological drama. The infancy narrative anticipates Jesus' identity as Emmanuel, "God with us." The ministry in Galilee reveals the inbreaking of the kingdom of heaven, marked by healing, teaching, and authority over nature. The growing opposition from religious leaders propels the narrative toward the climactic confrontation in Jerusalem. The passion story, far from being a tragic end, is presented as the necessary fulfillment of Scripture and the decisive act of God's salvation. The resurrection, unique in its Matthean emphasis on worship and mission, provides the resolution of the plot by commissioning disciples to continue the story.

Literary Artistry and Symbolism

Matthew's Gospel is not only a theological narrative but also a work of literary artistry. The use of fulfillment quotations provides a running commentary that links Jesus' actions with the larger scriptural story. The structuring of Jesus' teachings into five major discourses mirrors the five books of the Torah, inviting readers to see continuity between Moses and Jesus. Symbolic motifs (e.g., light and darkness, bread and wine, sheep and shepherds) recur throughout the narrative, creating thematic coherence.

This artistry underscores the Gospel's communicative strategy. Matthew does not merely present information. Instead, he shapes a narrative that evokes recognition, challenges assumptions, and calls readers into discipleship. Its literary form is inseparable from its theological message.

Conclusion

The Gospel of Matthew is best understood as a theological biography, a narrative that draws on the conventions of ancient *bioi* while reworking them to proclaim Jesus as Messiah, Son of God, and the teacher of righteousness. Its narrative strategies such as plot structure, characterization, symbolic geography, and literary motifs create a richly textured account that continues to speak powerfully to readers. Appreciating Matthew as literature enables interpreters to see not only what the Gospel says, but how it says it, and why its story continues to shape the faith and practice of the church.

Chapter 6
The Structure of Matthew

The structure of Matthew's Gospel has long been the subject of scholarly debate. How one discerns the arrangement of the Gospel is not merely a technical question but a window into the evangelist's theological intentions. While the Gospel clearly follows a broad chronological outline from Jesus' birth to his passion, death, and resurrection, its internal organization displays a careful balance of narrative and discourse. This literary design helps shape the Gospel's portrayal of Jesus as both teacher and Messiah.

Proposals for the Overall Structure

Scholars have proposed a variety of ways to outline Matthew, each illuminating different aspects of the Gospel's design.

One of the simplest approaches is to view the Gospel in two major halves: the Galilean ministry (chapters 1–16) and the Jerusalem passion and resurrection (chapters 17–28). This model highlights the geographical and thematic movement from revelation in Galilee to confrontation and fulfillment in Jerusalem. The turning point is often located at Peter's confession at Caesarea Philippi (16:13–20), where Jesus' identity is confessed and his path to suffering is first announced. This twofold scheme emphasizes the trajectory of Jesus' mission as one that moves from proclamation to passion.

A second approach sees Matthew in terms of a three-part structure. In this view, the Gospel begins with preparation and beginnings (1:1–4:16), moves into the central body of Jesus' teaching and ministry (4:17–25:46), and concludes with the climactic passion and resurrection (26:1–28:20). The key to this outline is the formula statement "From that time Jesus began..." (4:17; 16:21), which occurs twice and divides the Gospel into distinct sections. This scheme emphasizes turning points in Jesus' mission: the start of his proclamation in Galilee and the beginning of his journey toward the cross.

A third and widely discussed model focuses on the alternation of narrative and discourse. According to this pattern, Matthew organizes his Gospel into five major narrative units (chapters 3–4; 8–9; 11–12; 14–17; 19–23), each followed by a discourse (chapters 5–7; 10; 13; 18; 24–25). The pattern is reinforced by a recurring conclusion formula ("When Jesus had finished saying these things...") which marks the end of each discourse. Many interpreters connect this fivefold structure with the Torah, suggesting that Matthew intentionally presents Jesus as a new Moses who delivers God's definitive teaching in a manner parallel to the five books of Moses. This outline emphasizes Matthew's literary artistry and theological purpose, showing that the Gospel is carefully constructed rather than loosely arranged.

Other proposals attempt to discern chiastic patterns or concentric structures in Matthew. For example, some scholars argue that the Gospel as a whole forms an *inclusio*, beginning with the promise of "God with us" (1:23) and ending with the risen Christ's assurance, "I am with you always" (28:20). Others suggest that the central section of Matthew (chapters 13–17) functions as a literary and theological midpoint, with themes of parables, transfiguration, and discipleship forming the hinge of the narrative. While such proposals vary in detail, they underscore the conviction that Matthew is a carefully ordered composition in which placement and sequence carry interpretive weight.

Taken together, these structural models highlight different dimensions of Matthew's Gospel. The two-part outline stresses the movement toward Jerusalem; the three-part scheme highlights decisive turning points; the five-discourse model underscores Jesus as the new Moses; and chiastic readings bring attention to the Gospel's literary unity. No single proposal captures every nuance, but each contributes to a richer understanding of Matthew's design and purpose.

The Five Discourses

A distinctive feature of Matthew is its arrangement of Jesus' teaching into five major discourses, each introduced by narrative context and concluded with a formula such as "When Jesus had finished saying these things..." (7:28; 11:1; 13:53; 19:1; 26:1). Many interpreters see here a deliberate parallel to the five books of the Torah, suggesting that Matthew presents Jesus as a new Moses who delivers God's definitive instruction.

The five discourses are:

- *The Sermon on the Mount* (chapters 5–7): a foundational exposition of the kingdom, emphasizing righteousness, the law's fulfillment, and the character of discipleship.
- *The Mission Discourse* (chapter 10): instructions to the disciples as they are sent out, underscoring the demands and costs of mission.
- *The Parables Discourse* (chapter 13): a collection of parables revealing the mysteries of the kingdom, emphasizing both its hiddenness and inevitability.
- *The Community Discourse* (chapter 18): teaching on humility, forgiveness, and the life of the church as a community of disciples.
- *The Eschatological Discourse* (chapters 24–25): Jesus' apocalyptic teaching on the end of the age, the coming of the Son of Man, and the need for vigilance.

By organizing his material in this way, Matthew gives shape to Jesus' teaching ministry and highlights the continuing relevance of his instruction for the life of the community.

Narrative Flow

Between the discourses, Matthew's narrative moves forward with deliberate pacing. The infancy narratives (chapters 1–2) introduce Jesus as the fulfillment of Israel's story, setting a tone of continuity and fulfillment. The Galilean ministry (chapters 3–16) portrays the proclamation of the kingdom in word and deed, interwoven with increasing conflict with religious leaders. The turning point comes with Peter's confession at Caesarea Philippi (16:16), where Jesus is identified as "the Christ, the Son of the living God." From this moment, the narrative anticipates the passion, as Jesus predicts his suffering and the journey turns toward Jerusalem. The final chapters (26–28) slow the narrative pace, devoting disproportionate space to the passion and resurrection, underscoring their theological centrality.

Theological Implications of Structure

Matthew's structure is not accidental but deeply theological. The alternation of narrative and discourse portrays Jesus as both revealer and teacher. The five-discourse pattern links him with Moses and presents his words as covenantal instruction. The narrative progression from Galilee to Jerusalem reflects both geographical movement and theological climax, showing that the way of the Messiah leads inevitably to suffering, death, and vindication.

The structure thus functions pedagogically. It offers disciples both the story of Jesus and the teaching by which to live. Matthew provides not only a narrative to be believed but also instruction to be practiced, embodying the very emphasis on righteousness that pervades the Gospel.

Conclusion

The structure of Matthew reveals a Gospel carefully crafted to present Jesus as Messiah, teacher, and Lord. Through its alternation of narrative and discourse, its fivefold arrangement of teaching, and its climactic journey from Galilee to Jerusalem, the Gospel offers a literary design that serves theological ends. Recognizing this structure enables interpreters to perceive Matthew not as a random compilation of stories and sayings, but as a deliberate and coherent testimony to the meaning of Jesus Christ.

Chapter 7
Matthew's Use of the Old Testament

Few features of Matthew's Gospel are more striking than its pervasive use of the Old Testament. From the opening genealogy to the climactic resurrection narrative, Matthew consistently frames the story of Jesus as the fulfillment of Israel's Scriptures. This hermeneu-tical strategy is not merely decorative; it is central to the evangelist's theological vision. By weaving Scripture into nearly every major scene, Matthew presents Jesus as the embodiment of Israel's hopes and the climax of God's saving plan.

Formula Quotations and Fulfillment Motifs

One of Matthew's most distinctive literary devices is the use of formula quotations that are explicit citations of the Old Testament introduced with phrases such as "This was to fulfill what was spoken by the prophet..." (e.g., 1:22; 2:15; 2:23; 4:14; 8:17). These formula quotations punctuate the narrative at key junctures, serving as interpretive commentaries that guide the reader's understanding of Jesus' identity and mission.

For example, the infancy narratives are framed by multiple fulfillment quotations: the virgin conception recalls Isaiah 7:14 (1:23), the flight to Egypt echoes Hosea 11:1 (2:15), and the lament at Bethlehem invokes Jeremiah 31:15 (2:18).

Together, these texts anchor Jesus' birth in the history of Israel and present him as the one in whom the Scriptures reach their *telos* (i.e., fulfillment). Later, Matthew applies Isaiah 53:4 to Jesus' healing ministry (8:17), casting his works of compassion as signs of God's saving power.

These formula quotations reflect Matthew's conviction that Scripture is not static but dynamically fulfilled in the life of Jesus. The evangelist does not treat the Old Testament merely as prediction and its fulfillment as mechanical correspondence; rather, he interprets Scripture typologically, showing how Israel's story finds deeper meaning in Christ.

Typology and Figural Reading

Beyond explicit quotations, Matthew makes extensive use of typology, presenting Jesus as the fulfillment of Old Testament figures and events. The infancy narrative portrays Jesus as a new Moses. And so, like Moses, he is threatened by a murderous king, preserved in Egypt, and leads God's people into a new covenantal reality. The Sermon on the Mount, which is taught from a mountain, further reinforces this Mosaic imagery, suggesting that Jesus is the new lawgiver who brings Torah to its completion.

Typology also shapes Matthew's portrayal of Israel and the church. The temptation narrative in the wilderness (4:1–11) mirrors Israel's testing during the Exodus, but where Israel failed, Jesus remains faithful. The parables of the vineyard (21:33–46) and the wedding banquet (22:1–14) reinterpret Israel's history, placing Jesus at the center of God's covenantal purposes and portraying the community of disciples as the faithful remnant.

Such figural reading demonstrates Matthew's conviction that Scripture is a living word whose meaning expands in light of God's decisive action in Jesus.

Other Jewish Hermeneutical Methods

Matthew's engagement with the Old Testament also reflects interpretive techniques that were common within Second Temple Judaism. His handling of Scripture shows both continuity with Jewish exegetical practices and the distinctiveness of his Christ-centered reading.

One such method is midrashic interpretation, in which a biblical text is explained or reapplied to a new situation. Midrash often involves expanding a passage's meaning through wordplay, narrative elaboration, or thematic association. Matthew's creative use of Hosea 11:1 ("Out of Egypt I called my son") in reference to the holy family's return from Egypt (2:15) exemplifies this approach. In its original context, the verse refers to Israel's exodus, but Matthew reapplies it to Jesus, thereby portraying him as the embodiment of Israel's story.

Another practice that Matthew's Gospel seems to reflect is pesher-style interpretation, known from the Qumran community. Pesher interprets biblical prophecy as directly fulfilled in contemporary events, often introduced with a

formula such as "the interpretation of this is...."
While Matthew does not use this formula, his
repeated use of fulfillment citations functions in a
similar way, reading Israel's Scriptures as pointing
directly to events in the life of Jesus. The infancy
narrative, filled with such proof-texting, is perhaps
the clearest example.

Matthew also demonstrates a sensitivity to
intertextual echoes and the combination of texts,
another characteristic feature of Jewish hermeneutics. For instance, his presentation of Jesus'
triumphal entry into Jerusalem (21:4–5) weaves
together Zechariah 9:9 and Isaiah 62:11. This
practice of "stringing pearls" (joining multiple
texts) shows that Matthew did not regard Scripture
as a set of isolated passages but as a coherent whole
that bore witness to Jesus.

These methods highlight Matthew's dual
identity as both faithful heir of Jewish interpretive
traditions and bold innovator. His hermeneutic is
deeply Jewish in form but distinctively Christian in
content, because all readings converge on Jesus as
Messiah. What for other Jewish interpreters might
have been open-ended possibilities for fulfillment,
Matthew presents as finding their definitive
realization in the life, death, and resurrection of
Christ.

Key Theological Themes

Matthew's use of the Old Testament serves
several major theological themes. First, Matthew's
use of Scripture underscores Jesus' identity as
Messiah and Son of David. The genealogy (1:1–17)

anchors him in Israel's royal line, connecting him to David and Abraham. Fulfillment citations reinforce this messianic role, as when the crowds hail Jesus with royal acclamations during his entry into Jerusalem (21:4–9). Matthew thus portrays Jesus not as a break with Israel's past but as the heir to its deepest promises.

Second, Matthew presents Jesus as Emmanuel, "God with us." From the infancy narrative's citation of Isaiah 7:14 (1:23) to the risen Christ's final promise, "I am with you always" (28:20), the Gospel frames Jesus' life and ministry as the presence of God dwelling among his people. This Emmanuel theme assures readers that the God of Israel has not abandoned them but is faithfully present in Christ.

Third, Matthew develops the image of Jesus as the new Moses, the authoritative teacher who brings God's definitive instruction. Like Moses, Jesus comes out of Egypt (2:15), ascends a mountain to deliver covenantal teaching (5:1–2), and interprets the law as the foundation for God's people. The structuring of Jesus' teaching into five major discourses further echoes the five books of the Torah, reinforcing the claim that Jesus embodies and surpasses Moses as the ultimate lawgiver and mediator of God's will.

Other themes flow from these central motifs. Matthew's hermeneutic emphasizes fulfillment: Jesus does not abolish the law or the prophets but brings them to their intended goal (5:17). The Gospel also highlights the interplay between Israel and the nations, showing that while Jesus' mission begins with Israel, it extends to all peoples through the Great Commission (28:18–20). Finally, Matthew's scriptural interpretation sustains his vision of the kingdom of heaven and the ethic of righteousness that characterizes discipleship, grounding Christian life in continuity with Israel's Scriptures.

Together, these themes demonstrate that Matthew's use of the Old Testament is not peripheral but central. By portraying Jesus as Messiah, Emmanuel, and new Moses, and by framing his mission as the fulfillment of Israel's story for both Israel and the nations, Matthew presents Scripture as the indispensable key to understanding the significance of Christ.

Conclusion

Matthew's Gospel cannot be understood apart from its deep engagement with the Old Testament. Through formula quotations, typology, and interpretive methods rooted in Jewish tradition, Matthew portrays Jesus as the one in whom the Scriptures find their fulfillment. This hermeneutical strategy is central to Matthew's theological vision, ensuring that the story of Jesus is inseparable from the story of Israel. For readers of the Gospel, the Old Testament is not background but foreground and so is the essential canvas on which Matthew paints his portrait of the Messiah.

Part III
Matthew's Story

Chapter 8
Act 1
The Identity of Jesus Messiah
(1:1-4:16)

Having explored the historical background (Part I) and the literary shape and strategies of the Gospel (Part II), we now turn to Matthew's story itself. This part of the book offers a sequential reading of the Gospel, highlighting its narrative flow, literary features, and character development. Rather than treating Matthew only thematically or doctrinally, we follow the plot from Jesus' origins through his ministry in Galilee, his journey to Jerusalem, and his passion and resurrection. Along the way, we attend to Matthew's narrative artistry such as its structure, characterization, symbolism, and use of Scripture so that we can grasp how the Gospel tells its story and how that story communicates theological meaning.

Matthew's narrative unfolds in three broad acts: (1) the revelation of Jesus' identity, (2) the proclamation of his message and the varied responses it provokes, and (3) the path of suffering, climaxing in the passion, resurrection, and commissioning of the disciples. Each act draws readers more deeply into the drama of the kingdom of heaven, portraying Jesus as the Messiah and Son of God whose mission defines the meaning of discipleship and reveals God's saving purpose.

Origins and Divine Sonship (1:1–2:23)

Matthew begins with a genealogy (1:1–17), presenting Jesus as "the Messiah, the son of David, the son of Abraham." This genealogy is more than a family record; it is a theological claim. By tracing Jesus' lineage through Abraham, the father of Israel, and David, the paradigmatic king, Matthew establishes his messianic credentials. The structuring of the genealogy into three sets of fourteen generations underscores a sense of divine order in Israel's history, preparing for the climactic arrival of Jesus.

The infancy narratives (1:18–2:23) reinforce this identity with a series of fulfillment quotations. The virgin conception fulfills Isaiah 7:14 and underscores Jesus' divine origin as "God with us" (Emmanuel). The narratives also introduce a theme of conflict: Herod perceives Jesus as a rival king and seeks his destruction, prefiguring the opposition Jesus will face throughout his ministry. Meanwhile, figures such as Joseph, the Magi, and the angelic messengers embody faithful response, obedience, and divine guidance. Characterization here is especially important. Jesus is portrayed as both the climax of Israel's hopes and the object of resistance from earthly powers.

Preparation for Ministry (3:1–4:16)

The scene shifts from Bethlehem to the wilderness, where John the Baptist emerges as prophetic forerunner (3:1–12). His call to repentance and his announcement of one greater to come frame Jesus' appearance as the decisive moment in

God's redemptive plan. John is characterized as both faithful herald and figure of transition. His baptismal ministry prepares the way for Jesus but is surpassed by the one who baptizes with the Spirit and fire.

Jesus' own baptism (3:13–17) serves as a pivotal moment of divine confirmation. When Jesus submits to baptism, the heavens open, the Spirit descends like a dove, and the voice from heaven declares, "This is my Son, the Beloved, with whom I am well pleased." This trinitarian scene presents Jesus' sonship not merely as genealogical or royal but as divine vocation. The heavenly voice echoes Psalm 2:7 and Isaiah 42:1, linking kingship with the servant role, and thereby prefiguring a messiahship marked by both authority and suffering.

Immediately after, Jesus is led into the wilderness for testing (4:1–11). Here, the narrative explicitly links him with Israel's story, as he faces temptations echoing Israel's wilderness trials. Unlike Israel, however, Jesus remains obedient, countering each temptation with Scripture from Deuteronomy. His faithfulness establishes him as the true Son who embodies perfect obedience, and his resistance to Satan inaugurates the cosmic struggle that will unfold across the Gospel.

The section concludes with Jesus' withdrawal to Galilee (4:12–16). After John's arrest, Jesus relocates to Capernaum, fulfilling Isaiah's prophecy of light shining in the land of Zebulun and Naphtali. This brief notice functions as the hinge between preparation and proclamation. It confirms once again the theme of fulfillment and signals that Jesus' mission is the dawn of God's light breaking into a world of darkness.

Chapter 9
Act 2
The Proclamation of Jesus Messiah
(4:17-16:20)

Programmatic Beginning (4:17–25)

With John's arrest, Jesus steps into his public ministry. Matthew signals this transition with the programmatic declaration: "From that time Jesus began to proclaim, 'Repent, for the kingdom of heaven has come near.'" This statement summarizes Jesus' message throughout the Gospel: the reign of God, long anticipated in Israel's Scriptures, is now breaking into history through his ministry.

The calling of the first disciples (4:18–22) emphasizes the radical demands of following Jesus. Simon Peter, Andrew, James, and John immediately leave their nets, boats, and family to follow him. Their obedience exemplifies the reorientation demanded by the kingdom and introduces them as key figures who will embody both faith and failure.

The summary of ministry in 4:23–25 presents Jesus as authoritative teacher, herald of good news, and compassionate healer. His reputation spreads widely, and large crowds gather from diverse regions. The crowds' response is characterized by amazement and attraction, but their true allegiance remains ambiguous, foreshadowing the mixed responses that will dominate the rest of the Gospel.

Jesus the Authoritative Teacher
The Sermon on the Mount (5:1–7:29)

The Sermon on the Mount inaugurates Jesus' teaching ministry, portraying him as the new lawgiver who redefines righteousness for his followers. Delivered on a mountain, the discourse evokes Mosaic typology and establishes Jesus' authority over the Torah. The Beatitudes bless those who embody humility, mercy, and faithfulness, redefining the values of the kingdom.

The sermon emphasizes inward transformation as the fulfillment of the Law. Anger is equated with murder, lust with adultery, and love is extended even to enemies. Practices of piety (e.g., almsgiving, prayer, fasting) are critiqued when done for show and commended when done in secret before God. The Lord's Prayer centers the disciple's life on God's reign, provision, and deliverance. The discourse concludes with a call to obedience, likened to building a house on solid rock, and the crowds are astonished at Jesus' authority.

Through this discourse, Jesus is characterized as the authoritative teacher, the disciples as learners called to a higher righteous-ness, and the crowds as impressed but undecided. The theological heart of the sermon is the call to live as a community of righteousness that fulfills the Law through obedience shaped by love.

Authority in Action
Miracle Narratives (8:1–9:38)

After the sermon, Matthew portrays Jesus' authority in action through a series of miracle stories. These episodes, arranged in triads with interspersed discipleship sayings, reveal Jesus' power over sickness, nature, demons, and death. He heals the unclean, responds to the faith of a Gentile centurion, and restores Peter's mother-in-law, embodying compassion that crosses boundaries.

As the narratives progress, conflict begins to emerge. When Jesus forgives and heals a paralytic, scribes accuse him of blasphemy. Later, Pharisees charge him with casting out demons by demonic power. These episodes introduce the theme of opposition, even as the crowds marvel and disciples falter in understanding.

Interspersed are teachings on discipleship: the cost of following Jesus without delay, the calling of Matthew the tax collector, and the critique of empty ritual practices. These passages clarify that Jesus' authority summons more than admiration; it demands commitment. The section concludes with the image of Jesus as the compassionate shepherd, moved by the plight of the crowds and calling for laborers to join the harvest.

Mission and Conflict (10:1–12:50)

Jesus commissions the Twelve, granting them authority to heal and proclaim the kingdom. The Mission Discourse frames discipleship as active participation in Jesus' work, marked by both authority and suffering. The disciples are warned of persecution, division, and rejection, but they are assured of the Spirit's aid and the reward of perseverance.

Chapters 11–12 deepen the narrative of mixed responses. John the Baptist voices doubt from prison, the crowds remain fickle, and the Pharisees intensify their hostility. Controversies over Sabbath observance and exorcism crystallize the conflict. When Jesus is accused of collusion with Beelzebul, he declares that such rejection of the Spirit's work is unforgivable, exposing the gravity of opposition. Amid rejection, however, he also offers rest to the weary and burdened, embodying the gentleness of true messiahship.

In this section, disciples are portrayed as learners sharing in Jesus' mission, opponents are hardened in resistance, and the crowds remain caught between attraction and indecision. The kingdom of heaven is shown to provoke division, demanding allegiance and exposing the fault lines of human response.

Parables and Mixed Responses (13:1–16:20)

Chapter 13 collects parables that describe the kingdom's hidden yet unstoppable advance. The sower illustrates varied responses to the word; the weeds among the wheat emphasize patience until judgment; the mustard seed and yeast highlight small beginnings with great outcomes; and the pearl and treasure underscore the surpassing value of the kingdom.

Narrative episodes following the parables show this dynamic in action. Jesus is rejected in Nazareth, John is executed by Herod, and the disciples continue to oscillate between bold faith and confusion. Outsiders such as the Canaanite woman demonstrate remarkable faith, while insiders falter. Feeding miracles reveal Jesus' compassion, yet the disciples remain slow to grasp their meaning.

The section culminates at Caesarea Philippi with Peter's confession, "You are the Messiah, the Son of the living God." Jesus affirms the confession as divinely revealed and promises to build his church on this foundation. Yet the disciples' understanding is partial; they have grasped his identity but not yet the suffering that defines his mission. This incomplete recognition prepares the way for the turn toward Jerusalem in the next act.

Chapter 10
Act 3
The Passion and Resurrection of Jesus Messiah
(16:21-28:20)

The Journey toward Jerusalem (16:21–20:34)

With the formula, "From that time Jesus began to show his disciples..." (16:21), Matthew marks the narrative turn toward the cross. Jesus begins to predict his suffering and resurrection, but the disciples resist this revelation. Peter rebukes him, only to be rebuked in turn as a stumbling block. Jesus insists that discipleship requires self-denial and taking up the cross.

The Transfiguration offers a vision of glory that confirms Jesus' identity as the beloved Son, yet it too is framed by the necessity of suffering. Repeated passion predictions, disputes about greatness, and teachings on humility, forgiveness, wealth, and servanthood characterize this section. The parable of the laborers in the vineyard and the request of James and John underscore the kingdom's reversals: greatness is defined by service, not status.

The journey concludes with the healing of two blind men, who address Jesus as "Son of David" and follow him on the way. Their recognition and obedience stand in contrast to the disciples' faltering understanding and embody the pattern of true discipleship.

The Climax of Conflict in Jerusalem (21:1–25:46)

Jesus enters Jerusalem as a humble king, acclaimed by crowds yet they misunderstood the nature of his kingship. The cleansing of the temple dramatizes his challenge to the religious establishment, and confrontations with leaders dominate the narrative. Through parables of judgment and incisive debates, Jesus exposes their hypocrisy and silences their attempts to trap him.

Chapter 23 intensifies the conflict with a series of woes against the scribes and Pharisees, climaxing in Jesus' lament over Jerusalem. The temple is pronounced desolate, and judgment looms. The Olivet Discourse (chapters 24–25) sets present discipleship within the horizon of final judgment. Jesus warns of trials and false messiahs while exhorting vigilance and faithfulness. Parables of preparedness (e.g., the bridesmaids, the talents, and the sheep and goats) define discipleship as readiness expressed through acts of justice and mercy.

Here Jesus is characterized as prophet and judge, the disciples as learners preparing for mission, the crowds as passive observers, and the leaders as resolute opponents. The conflict has reached its peak, and the narrative now turns toward the passion.

The Passion Narrative (26:1–27:66)

The passion begins with Jesus announcing that the Passover is at hand and that the Son of Man will be handed over. The anointing at Bethany anticipates his burial, and the Last Supper reinterprets the covenant meal in terms of his body and blood. In Gethsemane, Jesus prays in agony, submitting to the Father's will, while the disciples fail to remain vigilant. Judas betrays him, Peter denies him, and all abandon him.

Trials before the Sanhedrin and Pilate expose both the leaders' hostility and Pilate's weakness. Jesus is mocked as king and crucified as a criminal, yet cosmic signs accompany his death: the temple veil is torn, the earth quakes, and tombs are opened. A Roman centurion confesses him as Son of God, ironically perceiving what others have missed. The women remain faithful witnesses at the cross and tomb, while the leaders futilely attempt to secure the grave with guards and a seal.

Jesus' death is portrayed as fulfillment of Scripture, the climactic act of obedient sonship, and the decisive revelation of his messianic identity.

The Resurrection and Commission (28:1–20)

The resurrection narrative vindicates Jesus and commissions his disciples. Women discover the empty tomb, encounter the risen Lord, and are sent as the first messengers. The guards report to the leaders, who fabricate a false account of theft, epitomizing futile opposition.

In Galilee, the disciples meet Jesus on a mountain. They worship him, though some doubt remains, a detail that underscores the realism of discipleship as a mixture of faith and hesitation. Jesus declares universal authority, commissions his followers to make disciples of all nations, and promises his abiding presence to the end of the age.

The Gospel thus concludes as it began, with Emmanuel, "God with us," framing the entire narrative with the assurance of divine presence.

Conclusion

Matthew's Gospel unfolds as a narrative drama in three acts, each deepening the reader's understanding of Jesus' identity and the meaning of discipleship. The first act presents Jesus' origins and preparation, revealing him as Messiah, Son of David, Son of Abraham, Emmanuel, and beloved Son. The second act depicts his proclamation of the kingdom in word and deed, his formation of a community of disciples, and the mixed responses of crowds, opponents, and followers, culminating in Peter's confession. The third act turns decisively toward the cross, where suffering, rejection, and death paradoxically reveal Jesus' identity as Son of God, vindicated in resurrection and commissioning his disciples for universal mission. The story begins with a genealogy and ends with a commission, framed throughout by the assurance of Emmanuel, "God with us."

Part IV
Thematic and Theological Concerns

Chapter 11
Christology in Matthew

Introduction

Christology forms the theological heart of the Gospel of Matthew. Every episode, discourse, and fulfillment citation is oriented toward answering the fundamental question: Who is Jesus? From the opening genealogy to the closing commission, Matthew presents Jesus as the fulfillment of Israel's story and the revelation of God's presence among humanity. His identity is unfolded through titles, actions, and relationships and each contributes to a portrait that is at once messianic, royal, prophetic, and divine.

Matthew's Christology is not presented abstractly but narratively. It emerges through Jesus' words and deeds, through the responses of disciples and opponents, and through the evangelist's pervasive use of Scripture. The titles Son of David, Son of God, Emmanuel, and Son of Man serve as interpretive keys, while his roles as teacher, healer, and judge reveal the scope of his authority. Together they express a Christology that is simultaneously rooted in Jewish expectation and open to universal mission.

Titles of Jesus in Matthew
Son of David

"Son of David" is the most explicitly messianic title in Matthew and functions as a bridge between Jewish hope and Christian confession. It appears in the opening verse of the Gospel (1:1), framing Jesus within the royal line of Israel's ideal king. The title recurs throughout the narrative in contexts of healing and mercy which includes the blind men crying out to the Son of David for sight (9:27; 20:30–31) and the Canaanite woman's appeal to him for her daughter's deliverance (15:22). These episodes reveal that the Davidic Messiah exercises his kingship through compassion rather than conquest. Matthew's portrayal thus transforms royal expectation concerning Jesus. His kingship is not political domination but merciful restoration and so is a reign that reaches beyond Israel to include Gentiles who recognize him by faith.

Son of God

The title "Son of God" pervades the Gospel and deepens Matthew's portrayal of Jesus' divine identity. It is declared at his baptism ("This is my beloved Son," 3:17), tested in the wilderness ("If you are the Son of God," 4:3, 6), confessed by disciples after the calming of the storm (14:33), and acknowledged by a Roman centurion at the cross (27:54). These moments trace a Christological arc from divine affirmation through temptation, revelation, and recognition.

For Matthew, "Son of God" expresses both relationship and role. It identifies Jesus as the obedient Son who fulfills Israel's vocation and as the one who uniquely reveals the Father's will. His authority to forgive sins, command nature, and judge the nations flows from this filial relationship. Yet Matthew's presentation remains thoroughly monotheistic: Jesus shares in God's authority and presence without erasing the distinction between Father and Son. The result is a relational Christology grounded in obedience and mission rather than in metaphysical speculation.

Emmanuel: God with Us

The name Emmanuel ("God with us") appears only in 1:23 and 28:20 but frames the entire Gospel. The birth narrative introduces Jesus as the divine presence incarnate in human history, while the closing commission reaffirms that presence as permanent and universal: "I am with you always, to the end of the age." Between these bookends, Matthew develops the theme of divine presence through Jesus' authority, compassion, and promise of abiding fellowship.

Emmanuel theology shapes every aspect of Matthew's narrative world. It grounds Jesus' healing ministry, legitimates his reinterpretation of Torah ("Where two or three are gathered in my name, I am there among them," 18:20), and sustains the community's mission in his physical absence. The presence of God once symbolized in the temple is now embodied in Jesus himself, making him both locus and mediator of divine presence.

Son of Man

The title "Son of Man," drawn from Daniel 7:13–14, is Jesus' preferred self-designation in Matthew and carries a rich complexity. It unites humility and exaltation, suffering and glory. On the one hand, the Son of Man has nowhere to lay his head (8:20) and will suffer rejection and death (17:12, 22). On the other, he has authority on earth to forgive sins (9:6) and will come in glory to judge the nations (25:31).

Matthew's use of the title underscores the paradox of Jesus' identity: he is the human representative who suffers and the divine judge who reigns. The "Son of Man" sayings move from present authority to future vindication, culminating in the passion and resurrection. In this way, Matthew integrates apocalyptic expectation with the story of Jesus' earthly ministry, presenting him as the one who embodies both the destiny of Israel and the sovereignty of God.

Messiahship and Kingship

Matthew's portrait of Jesus as Messiah centers on the redefinition of kingship. The genealogy and infancy narratives establish royal descent, but the story itself subverts expectations of power. The Messiah reigns from the margins as one born in poverty, threatened by Herod, and crucified under Roman authority. The entry into Jerusalem fulfills Zechariah's prophecy of a king who comes "humble and riding on a donkey" (21:5), and the passion narrative climaxes in a profound irony: the one mocked as "King of the Jews" truly is God's appointed ruler.

Matthew's theology of kingship is thus cruciform. Authority is expressed in service, and dominion is revealed through self-giving love. The final declaration of universal authority (28:18) affirms Jesus' kingship in resurrection, but it is a kingship defined by mercy, not coercion, and exercised through a community called to teach and serve.

Jesus as Teacher, Healer, and Eschatological Judge

Among the many titles and images Matthew employs, three roles most clearly express how Jesus embodies divine authority and presence: teacher, healer, and eschatological judge. These are not discrete functions but interwoven dimensions of his mission, revealing how the kingdom of heaven becomes visible in both word and deed.

As teacher, Jesus stands at the center of Matthew's theological vision. His teaching defines the shape of the kingdom and the character of those who belong to it. Matthew presents him as one who speaks with direct and unparalleled authority and not as a scribe dependent on tradition but as one who utters the very will of God. His words summon hearers to repentance, reframe the meaning of righteousness, and call for a life oriented toward mercy and justice. The Sermon on the Mount epitomizes this role. There, Jesus does not abolish the Law but discloses its true intent, moving from external observance to inner transformation. His parables further reveal his pedagogical method, inviting listeners into discernment rather than providing easy answers. The crowds respond with astonishment, but understanding belongs to those willing to follow and obey. Teaching, for Matthew, is therefore not merely instruction but revelation and so unveils divine wisdom through the voice of the Messiah.

As healer, Jesus manifests the compassion and restorative power of the kingdom. His miracles are not displays of wonder for their own sake but signs of God's reign breaking into a world marred by disease, impurity, and demonic oppression. Matthew consistently pairs Jesus' acts of healing with his teaching, presenting word and deed as mutually interpretive. In healing the leper, raising the dead, and feeding the multitudes, Jesus embodies Emmanuel, "God with us," not as a static title but as active presence. His authority extends over every realm of human brokenness, restoring both physical bodies and social relationships. The faith of those who approach him (which includes Gentiles, women, and the ritually unclean) becomes a recurring motif, demonstrating that the kingdom's mercy transcends traditional boundaries. In Jesus' touch, the marginalized find inclusion, and in his compassion, the divine character is revealed.

As eschatological judge, Jesus brings the story of divine revelation to its consummation. The same one who teaches mercy and performs healing will ultimately separate the faithful from the faithless. Matthew's Gospel holds together these seemingly divergent aspects of tenderness and judgment within a single vision of divine righteousness. In parables such as the weeds among the wheat and the net that gathers fish of every kind, judgment appears as the final disclosure of truth which is a necessary reckoning that completes the work of mercy. The climactic vision of the Son of Man enthroned in glory (25:31–46) portrays Jesus as the judge of all nations, whose criterion of judgment is the practice of compassion: feeding the hungry, welcoming the stranger, visiting the prisoner. In this way, judgment is not the negation of mercy but its vindication. The standard by which humanity is judged is the same mercy that Jesus has both taught and enacted.

In uniting these roles, Matthew portrays Jesus as the one in whom divine authority and human compassion converge. His teaching reveals the will of God, his healing enacts God's restoring power, and his judgment consummates God's justice. Each role reflects a facet of Emmanuel's presence: the God who speaks, the God who heals, and the God who judges. Yet all these facets are within the same person of Jesus, whose authority is exercised not through domination but through service, not through coercion but through truth and mercy.

Conclusion

Matthew's Christology is rich and multi-faceted, combining Jewish messianic expectation with the confession of divine presence. Jesus is the Son of David who fulfills royal hopes, the Son of

God who reveals the Father, the Emmanuel who embodies divine presence, and the Son of Man who unites suffering and glory. He teaches with authority, heals with compassion, and judges with righteousness. His kingship is humble yet cosmic, his authority both gracious and demanding.

Through this portrait, Matthew invites readers not only to confess Jesus' identity but also to participate in his mission. To recognize him as Messiah and Lord is to join the community that lives under his reign, embodies his mercy, and awaits his return.

Chapter 12
The Kingdom of Heaven

The kingdom of heaven stands at the center of Matthew's theological vision and functions as the primary framework for understanding Jesus' message and mission. From the opening proclamation, "Repent, for the kingdom of heaven has come near" (4:17), to the climactic parables and the final commission, Matthew presents the kingdom as the reality that defines all others. It is both the content of Jesus' teaching and the power at work in his deeds. It interprets his miracles, undergirds his ethics, and shapes his eschatology.

While the other Synoptic Gospels speak of the "kingdom of God," Matthew consistently uses the expression "kingdom of heaven." This distinctive phrasing does not indicate a different reality but reflects Matthew's Jewish reverence for the divine name and his concern to portray the kingdom as both transcendent and immanent and so shows God's reign breaking into the world through the person and ministry of Jesus. Understanding this kingdom is essential to understanding Matthew's theology, for it expresses not only what Jesus proclaimed but also who he is and what it means to follow him.

Defining the Kingdom of Heaven

In Matthew, the kingdom of heaven is not a geographic or political realm but the dynamic rule of God manifest in history. It refers to divine sovereignty rather than spatial territory and so the focus is on reign rather than the realm. This reign becomes visible wherever God's will is done, whether in the ministry of Jesus, in the life of the church, or in the final consummation at the end of the age.

The phrase carries deep roots in Israel's Scriptures, where God is celebrated as king over creation and as ruler of Israel. The prophets envisioned a day when God's kingship would be universally recognized and justice established among the nations. Matthew's Gospel proclaims that this eschatological hope has begun to be fulfilled in Jesus' ministry. When he heals the sick, forgives sins, and welcomes the outcast, the kingdom of heaven is already present and yet, its fullness still lies ahead.

Matthew's understanding of the kingdom therefore resists simple categorization as either "present" or "future." It is both; the kingdom is inaugurated but not yet consummated. Jesus' miracles and teachings are signs of the kingdom's presence, while his parables and eschatological discourses point forward to its completion. The tension between the "already" and the "not yet" pervades the Gospel, shaping both its theology and its ethics. Disciples live in the overlap of the ages: called to embody the values of the kingdom now, while awaiting its final manifestation when God's will is perfectly done on earth as in heaven.

The Kingdom in Word and Deed

Throughout the Gospel, Matthew pairs proclamation and action as two dimensions of the kingdom's reality. Jesus announces the kingdom in words and embodies it in deeds. His teaching defines the character of those who belong to it, while his miracles reveal its transformative power.

In the Sermon on the Mount, the kingdom is presented as a moral and spiritual order in which God's will shapes human life. The Beatitudes bless the poor in spirit, the meek, and the merciful as they are the ones who embody the kingdom's countercultural values. The prayer Jesus teaches his disciples ("Your kingdom come, your will be done") encapsulates the heart of Matthean discipleship. Jesus' disciples are to live in anticipation of the divine reign by enacting its justice and mercy in the present.

In his deeds, Jesus demonstrates that the kingdom is not merely an idea but a reality breaking into history. Healing the blind, cleansing lepers, and casting out demons are not isolated acts of compassion. They are, instead, eschatological signs that the age of God's rule has arrived. As Jesus declares in response to his critics, "If it is by the Spirit of God that I cast out demons, then the kingdom of God has come upon you" (12:28). The kingdom is therefore both proclamation and power, word and deed and so is a lived manifestation of divine sovereignty that renews creation and restores human wholeness.

Parables of the Kingdom

Matthew's collection of parables, especially in chapter 13, provides a sustained meditation on the mystery of the kingdom. The parables disclose both the nature of the kingdom and the varied responses it elicits.

The parable of the sower (13:1–23) introduces the central theme of mixed response: the seed is the same, but its fruitfulness depends on the soil. The kingdom's advance is neither automatic nor coercive; it invites hearing, understanding, and perseverance. The parable of the weeds among the wheat (13:24–30, 36–43) expands this idea by depicting a world where good and evil coexist until the final harvest. The community of the kingdom must therefore live with patience, trusting in divine judgment rather than seeking to uproot prematurely.

The mustard seed and the yeast (13:31–33) portray the kingdom's paradoxical growth: what begins small and hidden becomes great and pervasive. These images counter expectations of sudden triumph and reveal that God's reign advances through quiet transformation rather than overt conquest. The treasure and the pearl (13:44–46) emphasize the kingdom's surpassing worth, demanding total commitment. The net that gathers fish of every kind (13:47–50) mirrors the earlier parables of mixture and separation, reminding disciples that final judgment belongs to God.

Through these stories, Matthew teaches that the kingdom's nature is at once mysterious and assured. It advances despite opposition, grows from humble beginnings, and elicits radical devotion. The parables thus call disciples to faith, endurance, and discernment in the face of ambiguity.

Present and Future Eschatology

Matthew's Gospel holds together two temporal dimensions of the kingdom: its present reality in Jesus' ministry and its future consummation at the end of the age. This dual perspective shapes the Gospel's theology of hope, discipleship, and judgment.

In the present, the kingdom is manifested wherever Jesus acts and wherever his followers embody his teachings. The poor, the merciful, and the peacemakers already belong to it and its power is seen in acts of forgiveness and reconciliation. The church, therefore, lives as a community of anticipation, embodying the values of the coming reign in the midst of the world's brokenness.

Yet Matthew also looks forward to a decisive future when the kingdom will be revealed in fullness. The parables of judgment and the eschatological discourse (24–25) envision a time when the Son of Man will return in glory, and God's justice will prevail. This hope does not foster passive waiting but active faithfulness. The parables of the wise and foolish bridesmaids, of the faithful and slothful servants, and of the sheep and goats illustrate that readiness for the kingdom's consummation is demonstrated in deeds of love and mercy.

Matthew's eschatology is therefore ethical and participatory rather than speculative. The future kingdom casts its light backward into the present, shaping how disciples live now. The tension between present experience and future expectation sustains the moral seriousness of the Gospel. The grace that reveals God's reign also demands a righteousness that reflects it.

Conclusion

The kingdom of heaven is the thread that weaves together the Christological, ethical, and eschatological dimensions of Matthew's Gospel. It defines Jesus' identity as the one who inaugurates God's reign, reveals the shape of life under that reign, and points toward its ultimate fulfillment. The kingdom is both gift and demand. It offers forgiveness and transformation, yet it calls for repentance, obedience, and mercy.

For Matthew, to follow Jesus is to enter the kingdom's reality and to live already within the sphere of God's rule while awaiting its consummation. The kingdom is not a future escape but a present vocation, not a hidden doctrine but a lived experience of divine sovereignty in the midst of human history. Through the words and deeds of Jesus, the reign of heaven has drawn near, inviting all who hear to respond in faith, righteousness, and hope.

Chapter 13
Discipleship and the Church

Discipleship is central to Matthew's theological vision. More than any other Gospel, Matthew defines what it means to follow Jesus in a way that is not simply through individual devotion but as a shared way of life within a distinct community. The Gospel traces the disciples' journey from their initial call by the Sea of Galilee to their commissioning on a mountain in Galilee after the resurrection. Along the way, Matthew presents them as both models and mirrors for the reader and so they embody faith, misunderstanding, and eventual transformation.

At the same time, Matthew uniquely speaks of the "church" (*ekklēsia*), using the term explicitly in 16:18 and 18:17. The church is not a human invention, but the gathered community called into being by Jesus' authority and sustained by his presence. It is the living expression of the kingdom of heaven in history, where discipleship takes visible, communal form. This chapter explores Matthew's theology of discipleship and the nature of the church as the community of the kingdom.

The Portrait of the Disciples
Faith, Failure, and Restoration

Matthew's narrative portrayal of the disciples is marked by realism and tension. They are called, commissioned, and entrusted with Jesus' authority, yet they struggle repeatedly to understand his mission. Their journey encapsulates the paradox of discipleship in that the same faith that enables them to follow also exposes them to failure.

The calling of the first disciples (4:18–22) sets the pattern. Jesus' summons is abrupt and absolute: "Follow me, and I will make you fishers of men." The immediate response of leaving nets and family dramatizes the cost of discipleship for allegiance to Jesus takes precedence over all prior commitments. Yet this initial enthusiasm gives way to confusion as the Gospel progresses. When storms arise, they cry out in fear (8:26); when confronted with parables, they struggle to comprehend (13:36); and when Jesus speaks of suffering, they resist (16:22–23). Their faith is genuine but immature, needing the testing that the cross will bring.

Peter, as representative disciple, embodies this complexity. His confession at Caesarea Philippi ("You are the Messiah, the Son of the living God," 16:16) stands as the high point of recognition, yet his subsequent rebuke of Jesus reveals how easily faith can be distorted by human expectation. In the passion narrative, his denial of Jesus underscores the fragility of discipleship, while his later restoration anticipates the Gospel's message of renewal. For Matthew, failure is not the end of discipleship but the context in which grace restores and re-commissions.

The resurrection scene in 28:16–20 completes this arc. The disciples gather as commanded.

There, they worship, yet some doubt. This juxtaposition epitomizes Matthew's pastoral realism. Authentic discipleship exists amid uncertainty, sustained not by perfect understanding but by Jesus' abiding presence. The disciples' story thus mirrors the experience of Matthew's community which was a church learning to follow faithfully in the tension between belief and doubt, commission and weakness.

Community Instructions and the Way of Reconciliation (Matthew 18)

Matthew 18 stands as the central text for the Gospel's ecclesiology. Often called the "Community Discourse," it provides a theological charter for life within the *ekklēsia*. The discourse does not depict institutional structures but outlines spiritual relationships grounded in humility, care, and forgiveness.

The chapter begins with the disciples' question, "Who is the greatest in the kingdom of heaven?" (18:1). Jesus responds by placing a child in their midst, redefining greatness as humility and dependence. The true disciple is one who receives others with the same vulnerability and openness as a child. This teaching undermines hierarchical ambition and grounds community life in equality before God's mercy.

Jesus then warns against causing others to stumble and calls for radical self-examination: "If your hand or foot causes you to sin, cut it off" (18:8). The imagery is hyperbolic but serious. In essence, the disciples are responsible not only for their own integrity but for the spiritual well-being of others. The parable of the lost sheep (18:12–14) reinforces this ethic of care, portraying God's relentless pursuit of the one who strays. The church is to mirror this divine compassion, valuing every member as precious.

Verses 15–20 outline the process of reconciliation within the community. Conflict is inevitable, but restoration is always the goal. Private confrontation, small-group mediation, and finally appeal to the *ekklēsia* provide a graduated pattern aimed at repentance rather than exclusion. The promise that "where two or three are gathered in my name, I am there among them" situates reconciliation within the Emmanuel theology that pervades the Gospel. These teachings show that the risen Lord is present precisely where mercy and truth meet.

The discourse concludes with Peter's question about forgiveness and Jesus' reply through the parable of the unforgiving servant (18:21–35). Forgiveness, far from being optional, defines the community's very existence. The servant who receives mercy but refuses to extend it negates the grace that has freed him. For Matthew, the church lives by forgiveness. To withhold forgiveness is to deny the gospel itself.

The Great Commission and the Theology of Mission

The final scene of the Gospel (28:16–20) brings the themes of discipleship and community to their culmination. Here the disciples who once faltered are entrusted with Jesus' ongoing mission. The authority that has characterized Jesus' ministry ("he taught as one having authority," 7:29) is now shared with them: "All authority in heaven and on earth has been given to me. Go therefore and make disciples of all nations."

This commission redefines discipleship as a missionary vocation. To be a disciple is to make disciples, extending Jesus' presence and teaching to the ends of the earth. The triadic formula (i.e., baptizing "in the name of the Father and of the Son and of the Holy Spirit") situates the mission within the life of God, while the command to "teach them to obey everything I have commanded you" binds future discipleship to Jesus' own teaching. The final promise, "I am with you always," assures that the mission is sustained by Emmanuel's enduring presence.

Matthew's theology of mission thus flows directly from his Christology and ecclesiology. The church exists not for self-preservation but for participation in God's redemptive reign. Its authority is derivative, its power is service, and its witness is embodied obedience. The disciples' transformation from fear and failure to proclamation and faithfulness models the church's own vocation in the world.

The Great Commission also universalizes the scope of the kingdom. What began in Israel now extends to all nations, fulfilling the Abrahamic promise that through God's chosen people "all the families of the earth shall be blessed." Yet Matthew maintains continuity with Israel's story. The mission to the Gentiles does not replace Israel but realizes its intended vocation as a light to the nations.

Conclusion

In Matthew's Gospel, discipleship and the church are inseparable realities. To follow Jesus is to enter a community shaped by his teaching, sustained by his mercy, and commissioned for his mission. The disciples' journey from call to commission mirrors the church's ongoing story. They are the ones called by grace, formed through failure, reconciled by forgiveness, and sent to embody the kingdom's presence in the world.

The *ekklēsia* Matthew envisions is not a static institution but a dynamic fellowship of disciples living under the authority of the risen Lord. It is characterized by humility, care for the least, readiness to forgive, and fidelity to Jesus' commands. Through such a community, the promise of Emmanuel continues to be fulfilled and the assurance that the one who called and commissioned his followers remains present among them to the end of the age.

Chapter 14
Law, Righteousness, and Ethics

For Matthew, the kingdom of heaven is not only a matter of belief but of lived obedience. His Gospel offers the most sustained reflection among the Synoptics on the relation between Jesus and the Torah, on the meaning of righteousness, and on the ethical shape of life under God's reign. Jesus is portrayed as both faithful interpreter and eschatological fulfillment of the Law, the one who reveals its true intent and calls his followers to embody it through inner transformation and merciful action.

This chapter explores Matthew's theology of law and righteousness as the moral and theological core of his Gospel message. It considers how Jesus' teaching reconfigures the Torah, how his vision of righteousness exceeds conventional piety, and how his ethics integrates justice, mercy, and humility into a single vision of life in the kingdom.

Jesus and the Torah
Fulfillment and Reinterpretation

Matthew's Gospel presents a profound continuity between Jesus and the Torah, yet this continuity is also transformative. In 5:17–20, Jesus declares, "Do not think that I have come to abolish the Law or the Prophets; I have come not to abolish but to fulfill." This statement, unique to Matthew, is programmatic for the evangelist's ethical theology.

To "fulfill" does not mean merely to observe or complete but to bring to fullness which reveals the ultimate intention of the Law in light of God's eschatological purposes. Jesus embodies the Torah's deepest aims by internalizing its commands and centering them on love. He affirms the permanence of the Law ("not one stroke of a letter will pass away") while simultaneously calling his disciples to a righteousness that surpasses that of the scribes and Pharisees. The contrast lies not in the rejection of Torah but in its radicalization: what was external becomes inward; what was formal becomes relational.

The antitheses that follow (5:21–48) illustrate this interpretive fulfillment. Jesus reinterprets prohibitions on murder, adultery, and falsehood to expose the anger, lust, and deceit that violate love's integrity. The call to love enemies and pray for persecutors (5:44) reveals the Law's ultimate purpose: to shape a people who reflect God's perfect mercy. In this way, Matthew portrays Jesus as the definitive interpreter of Torah. Jesus is the new Moses whose authority surpasses that of the scribes because it issues from divine sonship.

Yet fulfillment also entails transformation. The ceremonial and boundary-marking dimensions of the Law yield to the ethical and universal demands of love. Ritual purity gives way to inner purity; dietary distinctions are superseded by moral discernment (15:10–20). The Law's aim is realized not in a legal code but in a community whose conduct mirrors God's character.

Righteousness as the Way of the Kingdom

"Righteousness" (*dikaiosynē*) is one of Matthew's key theological terms, appearing more frequently here than in any other Gospel. It signifies right relationship with God expressed in right conduct toward others. For Matthew, righteousness is not a matter of mere rule-keeping but of wholehearted alignment with the will of God.

In the Beatitudes, those who "hunger and thirst for righteousness" are blessed, and those "persecuted for righteousness' sake" are promised the kingdom (5:6, 10). Righteousness, therefore, is both gift and vocation; the divine will is realized in human life through obedience and mercy. It has a social dimension as well as a personal one; it involves not only private piety but justice in community.

The phrase "your righteousness must exceed that of the scribes and Pharisees" (5:20) is not a call to greater legal precision but to deeper moral integrity. The scribes' righteousness was defined by external conformity; Jesus calls for inner wholeness. True righteousness arises from a heart transformed by love of God and neighbor.

Matthew warns, however, against false righteousness which is merely religious perform-ance motivated by self-display. In 6:1–18, almsgiving, prayer, and fasting are affirmed as genuine acts of devotion only when done "in secret," before the Father who sees in secret. The contrast between hypocrisy and sincerity defines the ethical vision of the kingdom. Thus, righteousness is authentic when it springs from humility and love rather than from the pursuit of reputation.

Righteousness also functions eschatologically in Matthew. It is the standard by which final judgment is rendered. In the parable of the sheep and goats (25:31–46), the righteous are those who enact compassion toward "the least of these." The same mercy that fulfills the Law becomes the criterion of eschatological reward. In essence, righteousness in Matthew bridges the present and the future, joining obedience and hope, faith and justice.

Ethics of Mercy, Justice, and Integrity

Matthew's moral vision is holistic as it integrates ethical action, inner disposition, and social responsibility under the reign of divine mercy. Jesus' critique of the religious leaders centers precisely on their failure to unite these dimensions. "Woe to you, scribes and Pharisees, hypocrites! For you tithe mint, dill, and cumin, and have neglected the weightier matters of the Law: justice and mercy and faith" (23:23). This verse succinctly articulates Matthew's ethical theology which emphasizes that the Law's true essence lies in the triad of justice, mercy, and faithfulness.

Mercy (*eleos*) occupies a special place in Matthew's ethic. The citation of Hosea 6:6, "I desire mercy, not sacrifice" (9:13; 12:7), functions as a hermeneutical key to Jesus' moral teaching. Mercy expresses the heart of God and thus defines the life of the disciple. Acts of compassion toward the poor, forgiveness of enemies, and inclusion of outsiders are not optional virtues but manifestations of the kingdom itself.

Justice (*krisis*) is likewise central. It denotes not only fair judgment but restorative action on behalf of the oppressed. Matthew's Jesus demands integrity in social and economic life, confronting hypocrisy and exploitation. The parables of stewardship (24:45–25:30) depict accountability as a measure of faithfulness. Therefore, disciples are stewards of grace and must act accordingly.

Finally, integrity (*haplotēs* in concept if not terminology) ties Matthew's ethics together. The command to let one's "yes" be yes and "no" be no (5:37) calls for transparency of word and deed. Hypocrisy is the antithesis of kingdom ethics, while sincerity unites inner motive and outward action.

These dimensions converge in the ethical summary Jesus gives in 22:37–40: love of God and love of neighbor. On these two commandments "hang all the Law and the Prophets." The love commandment does not abolish Torah but provides its interpretive center. The righteousness of the kingdom, therefore, is not a new legalism but the renewal of life in love.

Conclusion

Matthew's theology of law and righteousness presents Jesus as the living fulfillment of Torah and his disciples as participants in its ongoing realization. The Law is neither negated nor rigidly preserved. Instead, it is transformed in the light of Jesus' person and teaching. Righteousness exceeds legality because it arises from the heart, and ethics transcends rule-following because it reflects divine mercy.

In this Gospel, righteousness and mercy are inseparable. The one who fulfills the Law calls his followers to embody the same justice and compassion that define God's own character. The ethics of the kingdom is thus relational rather than transactional, grace-filled rather than merit-based. To live righteously is to live mercifully; to live mercifully is to participate in the perfection of the Father, "who makes his sun rise on the evil and on the good" (5:45).

Matthew's vision of the Law culminates not in prohibition but in invitation. That invitation is to become a people whose lives reveal God's righteousness on earth as in heaven.

Chapter 15
Conflict and Opposition

Conflict pervades Matthew's Gospel from the moment of Jesus' birth to his crucifixion. Herod seeks to destroy him as an infant, the religious leaders oppose him in his ministry, and the crowds who once hailed him as Son of David later call for his death. Yet this opposition is never merely historical; it is theological. In Matthew's narrative world, resistance to Jesus reveals the tension between the kingdom of heaven and the kingdoms of this world.

Matthew's account of conflict operates on multiple levels. It is social and political, involving the confrontation between prophetic truth and institutional power; it is religious, engaging divergent interpretations of the Law and covenant; and it is cosmic, reflecting the clash between God's reign and the forces of evil. The evangelist writes not to vilify opponents but to interpret their opposition within the larger drama of salvation history. The rejection of Jesus fulfills Scripture and exposes the depth of human blindness, while the persistence of opposition after the resurrection frames the church's own experience in the world.

Portraits of Pharisees, Scribes, and Other Opponents

Matthew's portrayal of opponents is both detailed and theologically charged. Among them, the Pharisees and scribes occupy the most prominent role. They appear early in the narrative as representatives of religious authority and become the primary antagonists in Jesus' public ministry.

The Pharisees are depicted not as caricatures of hypocrisy but as embodiments of a flawed righteousness because they are zealous for the Law yet blind to its heart. Their concern for ritual precision and external conformity contrasts with Jesus' insistence on inward purity and mercy. The controversy over Sabbath observance (12:1–14) illustrates this clash. While the Pharisees interpret Sabbath law in terms of restriction, Jesus interprets it in terms of restoration, declaring himself "Lord of the Sabbath." Similarly, debates about purity (15:1–20) reveal opposing hermeneutics in that Jesus locates defilement not in dietary practices but in the intentions of the heart.

The scribes, often linked with the Pharisees, serve as interpreters of Torah and preservers of tradition. Their role is ambiguous for though they sit on "Moses' seat" (23:2) and thus carry legitimate authority, their conduct fails to embody what they teach. Matthew's seven woes in chapter 23 constitute both judgment and lament. The charges of hypocrisy, blindness, and self-exaltation are not merely moral critiques but prophetic indictments because those entrusted with interpreting God's word have obscured its truth through pride and legalism.

Other opponents include the Sadducees, who deny resurrection and confront Jesus with theological puzzles (22:23–33), and the chief priests and elders, who plot against him out of fear for their power (21:45–46). Herod Antipas represents the political dimension of opposition. He is a ruler whose moral weakness mirrors the corruption of worldly authority. Collectively, these figures embody what Matthew understands as resistance to divine revelation because they embody the refusal to recognize the new work of God in Jesus.

The Function of Conflict in Matthew's Narrative

Conflict in Matthew is not simply opposition for its own sake. Instead, it serves a revelatory and pedagogical function. Through confrontation, Jesus' identity and authority are clarified, and the true nature of the kingdom is made known. The escalating disputes with the religious leaders form a narrative and theological progression: from questioning and suspicion (9:1–13), to open accusation (12:24), to plotting Jesus' death (12:14), and finally to crucifixion (27:1–2).

Each controversy functions as a test case for the interpretation of Torah and the embodiment of righteousness. Questions about fasting, Sabbath, purity, and authority provide occasions for Jesus to articulate the kingdom's values. His responses consistently redirect attention from external compliance to internal transformation, from ritual to mercy, from human status to divine purpose.

Opposition thus becomes a means of revelation in that the rejection of Jesus exposes the inadequacy of the old order and highlights the newness of his message.

At the same time, conflict reveals the cost of discipleship. Those who follow Jesus share in his rejection. The Mission Discourse (10:16–25) prepares disciples for persecution, framing opposition as a sign of fidelity rather than failure. "If they have called the master of the house Beelzebul, how much more will they malign those of his household?" (10:25). The disciples' suffering participates in Jesus' own, transforming persecution into witness.

Polemics and Post-70 Jewish-Christian Relations

Matthew's sharp polemics against the Pharisees and scribes must be read within the historical and social context of the late first century, after the destruction of the Jerusalem Temple in 70 CE. In this period, both emerging rabbinic Judaism and the Matthean community were engaged in defining their identities apart from the temple and reinterpreting Israel's story in light of loss and renewal.

The conflicts depicted in the Gospel likely mirror intra-Jewish debates rather than external hostilities. Matthew's community remained deeply Jewish in theology, Scripture, and practice, yet it confessed Jesus as the fulfillment of Israel's hope. The harsh rhetoric of chapter 23, therefore, reflects the pain of separation within a shared religious world. It is a conflict between siblings, not strangers and so is an argument within the family of Israel about the meaning of covenant faithfulness.

Recognizing this context is crucial for responsible interpretation. Matthew's critique of the Pharisees should not be read as anti-Jewish but as an intra-Jewish prophetic denunciation of hypocrisy and hardness of heart. His polemics echo those of the Hebrew prophets, who condemned injustice and formalism within their own people. The "woes" of chapter 23, though severe, arise from lament as much as judgment. They culminate in Jesus' sorrowful cry over Jerusalem, "How often I desired to gather your children together…but you were not willing" (23:37).

For Matthew, the rejection of Jesus by the leaders is not the rejection of Israel as a whole. The Gospel continually depicts faithful Israelites (e.g., Joseph, the Magi, John the Baptist, Mary Magdalene, and the first disciples) as participants in God's purposes. The church's mission to "all nations" (28:19) is not a replacement of Israel but the expansion of its calling.

Woes and Judgment Oracles

Matthew's most concentrated expression of conflict is found in the series of woes in chapter 23. These speeches, while polemical, reveal the moral and theological core of Jesus' confrontation with religious authority.

The first group of woes (23:13–22) exposes the leaders' hypocrisy: they close the kingdom to others, exploit converts, and manipulate oaths. The second group (23:23–28) denounces their moral inversion because they are meticulous in tithing herbs yet neglectful of justice, mercy, and faith. The final woes (23:29–36) situate their actions within Israel's history of rejecting the prophets, culminating in the pronouncement that "all this will come upon this generation."

These oracles function as both critique and disclosure. They unveil the blindness of religious self-righteousness and the tragic irony of resisting the very God one claims to serve. Yet they also reveal the divine pathos: judgment is the consequence of spurned mercy. The lament that follows (23:37–39) transforms polemic into prophecy, giving voice to divine sorrow over human rebellion.

In the broader structure of the Gospel, the woes anticipate the eschatological judgment discourse of chapters 24–25. The moral failures of Israel's leaders foreshadow the fate of all who reject the kingdom's call. Conflict, therefore, is not merely historical but paradigmatic. Conflict in Matthew's Gospel is an ongoing contest between self-justifying religiosity and the righteousness of mercy that Jesus embodies.

Conclusion

Matthew's theology of conflict reveals the paradox of divine revelation: God's truth provokes resistance even as it invites repentance. The opponents of Jesus are not villains for their own sake but mirrors of the human tendency to defend systems of power and piety against the unsettling demands of grace. In exposing their hypocrisy,

Matthew confronts every reader with the question of allegiance: will one cling to familiar forms of righteousness or embrace the disruptive mercy of the kingdom?

For the church, Matthew's portrait of conflict carries both warning and comfort. It warns that fidelity to Jesus will entail opposition, yet it comforts by framing such opposition within God's sovereign purpose. The same rejection that leads to the cross becomes the means of redemption, and the hostility of the world cannot nullify the promise of Emmanuel, "God with us."

Chapter 16
Passion, Death, and Resurrection

In Matthew's Gospel, the passion and resurrection of Jesus are not simply the conclusion of the narrative but the lens through which the entire story must be read. The themes that have shaped the Gospel (fulfillment, righteousness, the kingdom of heaven, and Emmanuel's presence) all converge here. Jesus' death is the revelation of divine kingship; his resurrection is the vindication of that revelation. Together they constitute the climax of the evangelist's theological vision: the kingdom of heaven arriving through suffering love and renewed through life beyond death.

The Passion as the Revelation of the Kingdom

Matthew presents the passion not as the failure of Jesus' mission but as its fulfillment. From the moment Jesus announces, "The Son of Man will be handed over to be crucified" (26:2), the narrative moves with solemn inevitability toward the cross. Every scene reveals that divine purpose unfolds precisely through human betrayal and injustice.

The setting of the Passover meal frames the death of Jesus as a redemptive event. When Jesus blesses bread and wine as his body and blood "poured out for many for the forgiveness of sins" (26:28), he interprets his impending death as covenantal sacrifice. The exodus from Egypt becomes the typological backdrop. Just as the blood of the lamb marked Israel's deliverance, so the blood of Christ secures liberation from sin and death. Matthew alone uses the phrase "for the forgiveness of sins," clarifying that the passion accomplishes what Jesus' ministry has foreshadowed: the healing and reconciliation of humanity with God.

The narrative of Gethsemane deepens this theology of obedience. Jesus' anguished prayer, "not as I will, but as you will," embodies the righteousness he has preached throughout the Gospel: wholehearted alignment with the Father's will. The disciples' failure to remain awake parallels humanity's inability to sustain faithfulness. Yet even their weakness becomes a space for grace, as Jesus' submission secures redemption for the unfaithful.

In the trials before the Sanhedrin and Pilate, Matthew underscores the paradox of divine justice as the innocent are condemned so that the guilty might be freed. Pilate's washing of hands dramatizes the futility of human attempts to evade moral responsibility, while the people's cry, "His blood be on us," ironically speaks truth. That blood has indeed come upon them, not as curse but as the very means of salvation. The passion narrative thus transforms political and religious conflict into theological revelation.

At Golgotha, the crucified Messiah reigns as king. The signs that accompany his death (darkness, earthquake, and the rending of the temple veil) are not embellishments but apocalyptic disclosures. Creation convulses as its Lord suffers; the barrier between God and humanity is torn open. Even the centurion's confession, "Truly this was the Son of God," signals that recognition of Jesus' identity now extends beyond Israel to the Gentiles. The kingdom of heaven has broken every boundary, even that between life and death.

Divine Purpose and Human Betrayal

One of Matthew's distinctive theological achievements is his capacity to hold divine sovereignty and human agency in tension. Judas' betrayal, the leaders' scheming, and Pilate's cowardice all serve divine purposes without excusing human guilt. The cross, for Matthew, is not an accident of history but the consummation of Scripture. Fulfillment formulas appear throughout the passion narrative (e.g., the thirty pieces of silver, the potter's field, the mockery of the soldiers) reminding readers that even human malice cannot thwart the divine plan.

This motif reveals Matthew's theology of providence: God's will is accomplished not in spite of human sin but through the transformation of it. The passion unveils the mystery of Emmanuel's presence in the deepest absence; God is with us, even in the experience of abandonment. Jesus' cry of dereliction ("My God, my God, why have you forsaken me?") is not a lapse of faith but the ultimate act of trust. Jesus addresses the God who seems absent precisely because he knows that presence is not lost.

Thus, the cross stands as both judgment and grace. It judges the false righteousness that resists mercy and exposes violence masquerading as piety. Yet it also reveals divine mercy as unbroken fidelity for the God who commands love of enemies now dies loving his own enemies. The kingdom of heaven is manifested not through conquest but through cruciform love.

The Resurrection as Vindication and Mission

If the cross is the revelation of divine love, the resurrection is its vindication. Matthew narrates the resurrection not primarily as proof of immortality but as the triumph of God's faithfulness. The same divine power that sustained Jesus in obedience now raises him in glory, confirming that righteousness leads not to defeat but to life.

The resurrection narrative (28:1–20) mirrors the passion in structure and tone. Cosmic imagery reappears (earthquake, dazzling angel, and fear) marking continuity between death and new creation. The angel's announcement, "He is not here; he has been raised," transforms absence into presence. The women's role as first witnesses embodies Matthew's recurrent theme that faithfulness and insight often come from the margins. Their worship at Jesus' feet contrasts with the guards' paralysis, dramatizing two possible responses to resurrection: adoration or fear, discipleship or denial.

The counter-story of the bribed guards (28:11–15) serves as narrative closure to the motif of opposition. Those who tried to secure the tomb now fabricate falsehood, demonstrating that unbelief persists even in the face of truth. Yet the Gospel's final word belongs not to deceit but to commission.

The climactic scene on the mountain in Galilee gathers all of Matthew's theology into one moment. Jesus' declaration, "All authority in heaven and on earth has been given to me," affirms that the crucified one now exercises universal sovereignty. The command to "make disciples of all nations" translates the passion into mission and so the forgiveness won through the cross becomes the message proclaimed to the world. Baptism into the triune name and obedience to Jesus' teaching unite identity and practice, theology and ethics. The final promise, "I am with you always," closes the circle begun with Emmanuel at his birth. The presence that entered the world in vulnerability remains with the church in glory.

Cross and Resurrection as a Single Revelation

In Matthew's integrated vision, cross and resurrection cannot be separated. The resurrection does not erase the cross but interprets it; the cross does not end in defeat but opens into the life of the resurrection. Together they reveal the paradoxical character of the kingdom. It is power manifested in weakness, glory hidden in humility, life emerging from death.

This unity shapes the moral and spiritual life of the disciple. The call to take up the cross (16:24) is now illuminated by resurrection hope. To follow

Jesus is to share his path of obedience, suffering, and vindication. Discipleship thus becomes participation in the divine pattern of death and life, loss and renewal. The church lives between these realities, bearing witness to the crucified and risen Lord by embodying his mercy and righteousness in the world.

Matthew's theology of the passion and resurrection is therefore profoundly pastoral. It speaks to a community facing persecution and uncertainty, assuring them that the presence of the risen Christ sustains them in the midst of suffering. The final words of the Gospel are not merely promise but identity. To be the church is to live under the continuing reign of Emmanuel, the crucified and risen Lord who remains with his people until the kingdom is complete.

Conclusion

The passion and resurrection in Matthew form a single revelation of divine righteousness. The cross unveils God's mercy; the resurrection confirms its power. In both, the kingdom of heaven is made visible not as distant realm, but as transforming reality within human history.

Matthew's narrative begins with the genealogy of a royal son and ends with the enthronement of that Son over all creation. The journey from Bethlehem to Golgotha, from emptying to exaltation, discloses the heart of God: a love that redeems through suffering, reigns through service, and endures through presence. The Gospel's final note, "I am with you always," is not epilogue but essence. The story of Jesus continues wherever his disciples live the pattern of his cross and proclaim the hope of his resurrection.

Part V
Interpretation and Reception

Chapter 17
Matthew in Early Christianity

From the first century onward, the Gospel of Matthew occupied a privileged place in the life of the early church. It was the most frequently cited of the four Gospels in the writings of the Apostolic Fathers, the most widely used in catechesis and worship, and the foundation upon which early Christian theology began to take literary form. Matthew's synthesis of Scripture, ethics, and Christology resonated deeply with the formative concerns of emerging Christian communities: continuity with Israel's story, moral transformation, and the presence of God in Christ.

This chapter explores how early Christian interpreters and communities received Matthew's Gospel not only as a record of Jesus' teaching, but as a living text that shaped doctrine, devotion, and practice. It considers three primary dimensions of that reception: patristic exegesis, liturgical and catechetical use, and the theological themes that made Matthew especially influential in the shaping of early Christian identity.

Patristic Exegesis and Theological Interpretation
The Apostolic Fathers and Early Witnesses

By the early second century, Matthew was already circulating widely across the Mediterranean. The *Didache* reflects Matthew's influence in its moral instruction ("the two ways") and in its version of the Lord's Prayer (8:2), echoing the Sermon on the Mount almost verbatim. Ignatius of Antioch cites Matthew's sayings about meekness, mercy, and confession of Christ before men. Polycarp and Barnabas both quote the Beatitudes, while 2 Clement interprets Matthew's ethical teachings as the rule of the new covenant community.

In these earliest writings, Matthew serves as a catechetical and ethical authority rather than a source for theological speculation. Its moral seriousness and emphasis on visible obedience appealed to communities defining themselves over against both Jewish and pagan environments. Jesus' words in Matthew 7:21, "Not everyone who says to me, 'Lord, Lord,' but only the one who does the will of my Father," became a watchword for authentic discipleship.

Irenaeus and the Fourfold Gospel

By the late second century, Irenaeus of Lyon established Matthew's place within the emerging fourfold canon. In *Against Heresies*, he insists that just as there are four corners of the earth and four winds, there must be four Gospels that begin with Matthew, which he calls the Gospel written for the Jews. Irenaeus regards Matthew's genealogy and fulfillment quotations as proof that Christ is the promised Messiah who recapitulates Israel's history. His appeal to Matthew's authority also functions polemically against Gnostic fragmentation. For Ireneaus, the Gospel embodies continuity, unity, and fleshly reality. In essence, the Gospel is "Emmanuel, God with us."

Origen and the Spiritual Sense

In the early third century, Origen of Alexandria advanced a method of reading Matthew that shaped Christian exegesis for centuries. His *Commentary on Matthew* combines philological precision with spiritual interpretation. For Origen, Matthew's literal sense reveals Christ's historical acts; its moral sense instructs the soul; and its spiritual sense unveils heavenly mysteries. The Sermon on the Mount, he argues, portrays the ascent of the soul toward perfection, moving from external obedience to inner transformation. Origen's allegorical readings of the parables, particularly the net and the pearl, established interpretive patterns that endured throughout the patristic era.

Chrysostom and Pastoral Preaching

In the late fourth century, John Chrysostom produced his celebrated *Homilies on Matthew*, the most extensive exposition of the Gospel in Greek antiquity. Preached in Antioch and later in Constantinople, these sermons reveal Matthew's continuing power to form Christian ethics. Chrysostom emphasizes the Gospel's moral realism in that discipleship is demanding but attainable through divine grace. His homilies on the Beatitudes interpret poverty of spirit and meekness as practical virtues, while his treatment of the Lord's Prayer unites piety and social responsibility. Through Chrysostom, Matthew became a manual for Christian living.

Matthew in Liturgy and Catechesis

The Gospel of Matthew quickly became central to the church's public and sacramental life. Its narrative coherence and ethical clarity made it the preferred text for catechetical instruction and liturgical reading.

Baptismal Catechesis

Because Matthew ends with the baptismal formula "in the name of the Father and of the Son and of the Holy Spirit" (28:19), it was naturally associated with baptismal preparation. Fourth-century catechists such as Cyril of Jerusalem and Ambrose of Milan expounded Matthew's baptism scenes to instruct catechumens in repentance and renewal. The Sermon on the Mount served as the moral charter for those preparing for the font and so was a program of conversion that joined doctrine to conduct.

The Lord's Prayer and Eucharistic Use

The Matthean form of the Lord's Prayer (6:9–13) became the church's standard liturgical text. Recited daily by the faithful and taught to the newly baptized, it expressed the communal ethos of dependence, forgiveness, and hope in God's coming reign. Likewise, Matthew's institution narrative (26:26–29) shaped the earliest Eucharistic prayers. The phrase "for the forgiveness of sins" entered the liturgical lexicon, grounding the sacrament in covenantal reconciliation.

Lectionary and Calendar

By the fourth century, Matthew was the dominant Gospel in the liturgical cycle of both East and West. The early Jerusalem lectionaries began the annual Gospel reading with Matthew 1 at the feast of Christ's birth, and the Western tradition often assigned Matthew's passion to Palm Sunday. In the monastic lectionaries, the Sermon on the Mount was read sequentially during Lent as preparation for Easter baptism. The Gospel thus framed the Christian year, narrating the rhythm of salvation from incarnation to resurrection.

Theological Themes in Early Reception

Christ as New Moses and Divine Teacher

Early interpreters frequently identified Matthew's Jesus with the new Moses. The five discourses were read as the new Pentateuch, the mountain as a new Sinai, and the Sermon on the Mount as the definitive law of the Spirit. For patristic writers, this typology preserved continuity with Israel while asserting the surpassing revelation of Christ. The new Moses theme also undergirded catechesis: just as Israel was formed by Torah, so the church is formed by Jesus' teaching.

Fulfillment and Unity of Scripture

Matthew's frequent fulfillment citations ("This took place to fulfill what was spoken by the prophet...") provided the hermeneutical foundation for Christian claims to the Old Testament. Fathers such as Justin Martyr and Irenaeus used these formulae to argue that the God of Israel and the Father of Jesus Christ are one and the same. Thus, Matthew anchored Christian identity in the continuity of salvation history, countering Marcionite and Gnostic dualisms.

Ethics and the Way of Life

Patristic ethics drew heavily from Matthew's moral vision. The Beatitudes, the call to love enemies, and the command to forgive became core features of Christian moral teaching. Tertullian appealed to the Sermon on the Mount in defending non-retaliation and truthfulness; Cyprian cited it in his treatise on the Lord's Prayer; Augustine later built his entire moral theology on its pattern. Matthew's union of righteousness and mercy shaped the ethos of early monasticism, where the Gospel's call to perfection (5:48) defined ascetic striving as participation in divine life.

Conclusion

In the first four centuries, Matthew's Gospel functioned as Scripture par excellence. The Gospel was understood as the text through which the church learned who Jesus is, how Scripture finds fulfillment in him, and how believers are to live. Its Christology affirmed divine presence; its ethic formed character; its liturgical use nurtured communal identity.

Through interpreters such as Ignatius, Irenaeus, Origen, and Chrysostom, Matthew became both theological foundation and moral compass. The Gospel's portrayal of Jesus as Emmanuel, the divine teacher who fulfills the Law and embodies mercy, offered early Christianity its grammar of faith and its pattern of life.

Matthew's voice thus continued to echo through the early centuries as both proclamation and practice: the Word made text for the Word made flesh.

Chapter 18
History of Interpretation

Across two millennia, the Gospel of Matthew has remained a mirror in which each age has seen its own reflection of the Christian life. Medieval monks, scholastic theologians, reformers, and modern critical scholars all turned to Matthew as both teacher and judge, finding in its words the measure of faith, morality, and truth. Few books of Scripture have exerted such continuous influence or generated such diverse interpretations.

This chapter surveys major developments in the interpretation of Matthew from the medieval through the modern periods, tracing how historical, ecclesial, and intellectual contexts shaped its reading. It focuses on three main epochs: the medieval synthesis of exegesis and spirituality; the Reformation's retrieval of grace and authority; and the emergence of modern scholarship, which re-situated Matthew within historical criticism, theology, and global interpretation.

Medieval Exegesis and Monastic Reading

In the Middle Ages, the Gospel of Matthew served as the cornerstone of both personal devotion and theological reflection. Its practical orientation and moral depth made it ideal for monastic meditation and scholastic commentary alike. Medieval interpretation assumed that Scripture contained multiple layers of meaning (i.e., the literal, allegorical, moral, and anagogical) all of which pointed to Christ and the Christian life.

Monastic Lectio Divina

In monastic settings, Matthew was read within the rhythm of prayer and liturgy rather than detached study. The Sermon on the Mount, in particular, was regarded as the monastic rule of life, embodying the Beatitudes that defined humility, purity, and mercy. Figures such as Gregory the Great and Bede the Venerable interpreted Matthew as a spiritual ladder ascending toward union with God. Gregory's *Homilies on the Gospels* treat Matthew's parables and miracles as allegories of the soul's transformation and each miracle an interior event in the believer's heart.

Scholastic Exegesis and the Harmony of Reason and Faith

With the rise of the medieval universities, commentary on Matthew became a vehicle for exploring the harmony between reason and revelation. Thomas Aquinas, in his *Catena Aurea* ("Golden Chain"), compiled the interpretations of the Fathers into a continuous commentary on Matthew. His synthesis exemplified scholastic theology's respect for tradition and its confidence that faith and intellect could coexist. The Beatitudes were interpreted as stages of sanctification culminating in the vision of God, while the Lord's Prayer was read as a summary of all Christian petition.

Popular Piety and the Medieval Imagination

Matthew also shaped medieval preaching, art, and drama. The parables of the Last Judgment, the Ten Virgins, and the Sheep and Goats dominated visual depictions of heaven and hell. In the mystery plays, Matthew's scenes of judgment and mercy educated the laity in the moral order of salvation. The Gospel's portrayal of Christ as judge and teacher structured medieval spirituality. Obedience, penitence, and almsgiving were understood as responses to the kingdom's demands.

Reformation Interpretations
Scripture, Grace, and Authority

The Protestant Reformation reoriented the reading of Matthew around questions of authority, grace, and obedience. While all reform movements affirmed Scripture's supreme authority, they diverged sharply in how they interpreted the demands of the Gospel, particularly the Sermon on the Mount. For some, Matthew revealed a moral ideal that drives believers to grace and faith; for others, it prescribed an attainable pattern of holiness, made possible by divine grace active within the believer.

Luther: Law, Gospel, and the Eschatological Ideal

Martin Luther's reading of Matthew was shaped by his fundamental distinction between Law and Gospel. He viewed the Sermon on the Mount as the most searching expression of divine law. In essence, this Sermon set a standard so pure that it exposes the depth of human sin and reveals the necessity of grace. "Be perfect, as your heavenly Father is perfect" (5:48) is not an achievable ethic but a mirror that reflects humanity's incapacity to fulfill divine righteousness apart from Christ.

For Luther, the Sermon's function is therefore pedagogical and evangelical: it humbles the sinner, magnifies Christ's mercy, and leads to justification by faith alone. Once justified, however, the believer begins to live out the spirit of the Sermon not to attain righteousness, but as a grateful response to it. The same Sermon that condemns self-righteousness also defines the shape of sanctified life. In this sense, Matthew's Gospel discloses both the terror of the Law and the comfort of the Gospel, revealing how God's impossible demand becomes possible through grace.

Calvin: Covenant, Kingdom, and the Sanctified Life

John Calvin shared Luther's conviction that salvation is by grace alone, yet his reading of Matthew gave more sustained attention to the ethical formation of believers. In his *Commentary on the Synoptic Gospels*, Calvin interpreted the Sermon on the Mount as Christ's authoritative exposition of the moral law for those already regenerated by the Spirit. The Law no longer condemns the faithful but instructs them in holy living; it functions not as a ladder to salvation but as a lamp for those walking in covenant fellowship with God.

For Calvin, the Sermon describes the life of the kingdom inaugurated by Christ. The Beatitudes mark the work of the Spirit within the church; the

Lord's Prayer teaches humility and dependence; the Great Commission defines the church's mission. While Luther read the Sermon primarily as an eschatological ideal, Calvin read it as a covenant ethic which depicts a concrete pattern of life under the reign of grace. Matthew thus became for Calvin the charter of a disciplined community shaped by both divine promise and moral responsibility.

Anabaptists: The Realized Ethic of the Kingdom

The radical reformers, by contrast, rejected any distinction between ideal and attainable righteousness. For them, the Sermon on the Mount was not a vision of perfection beyond human reach but the binding constitution of the true church. In documents such as the *Schleitheim Confession* (1527) and Menno Simons' *Foundation of Christian Doctrine*, Matthew's commands regarding nonviolence, truthfulness, enemy love, simplicity, and community discipline are taken as direct, literal obligations for disciples.

This "realized ethic of the kingdom" defined the Anabaptist understanding of the church as a visible, countercultural fellowship of believers. Baptism followed confession, not birth; coercion and violence were rejected as incompatible with Christ's lordship. In taking the Sermon at face value, the Anabaptists sought to restore the purity and immediacy of the early Christian community, where faith was enacted through obedience and the kingdom of heaven was already breaking into history.

Catholic Reform: Sanctification and the Imitation of Christ

The Catholic Reformation also drew deeply from Matthew but integrated its moral teaching within a sacramental and ecclesial framework. The *Spiritual Exercises* of Ignatius of Loyola invite meditation on Matthew's narrative of Jesus' ministry, emphasizing interior conversion that issues in active love. The Council of Trent affirmed the possibility of genuine sanctification: justification initiates a process of grace that transforms the believer's life. The Sermon on the Mount, far from being an impossible ideal, was proclaimed as the attainable goal of holiness through cooperation with grace and participation in the sacraments.

For the Catholic Reformers, Matthew united contemplation and action. The believer imitates Christ by practicing mercy, humility, and justice which are virtues that are both divine gifts and human responsibilities. The Gospel thus served as a manual for renewal: personal, communal, and ecclesial.

Synthesis: Two Reformation Trajectories

The Reformation era produced two enduring trajectories in the interpretation of Matthew. Luther and Calvin stressed the eschatological ideal of the Sermon on the Mount as depicting an ethic that confronts human sin and finds fulfillment only through grace. The Anabaptists and Catholic Reformers, by contrast, emphasized the realized ethic of sanctification and so saw it as an invitation to live the kingdom's values here and now through transformed lives and communities.

Together, these readings reflect the dialectic that has shaped Christian ethics ever since: Matthew's Gospel simultaneously humbles and empowers, proclaiming a righteousness that is both gift and vocation, both beyond reach and already at work in those who follow the crucified and risen Lord.

Modern Biblical Scholarship and Theological Interpretation

The modern era transformed the study of Matthew's Gospel more profoundly than any previous age. From the rationalist investigations of the Enlightenment to the pluralist voices of contemporary theology, interpreters have alternately dismantled and rediscovered Matthew's theological coherence. The Gospel that had once functioned primarily as the church's moral and liturgical manual now became a laboratory for historical reconstruction, literary theory, and ideological critique. Yet through these shifting methods, Matthew continued to provoke reflection on revelation, discipleship, and the presence of God in history.

Historical-Critical Inquiry and the Search for Origins

The Enlightenment ushered in a new confidence in reason and historical investigation. Scholars began to ask not only what Matthew meant for faith, but how it came to be. The eighteenth and nineteenth centuries thus witnessed the rise of source criticism, which sought to uncover the literary relationships among the Synoptic Gospels. The discovery of Markan priority (the view that Mark was written first and used by Matthew and Luke) along with the hypothesis of a sayings source (Q), reshaped the understanding of Matthew's composition.

In this context, Matthew came to be viewed not as an eyewitness record but as a theological redactor who reinterpreted inherited traditions for his community. The work of scholars such as Heinrich Holtzmann and later B. H. Streeter placed Matthew within a developmental model of early Christianity, emphasizing editorial purpose over direct apostolic memory.

Nineteenth-century liberal theology extended this inquiry to the figure of Jesus himself. Thinkers such as Albrecht Ritschl and Adolf von Harnack read Matthew as the Gospel of ethical monotheism, portraying Jesus as the supreme moral teacher who revealed the "Fatherhood of God" and the "brotherhood of man." The kingdom of heaven, in their hands, became an ethical ideal rather than an eschatological event. This moral domestication of Matthew mirrored the optimism of the age: revelation was assimilated into culture, and the radical demands of discipleship were softened into the progress of civilization.

While these approaches often stripped the Gospel of its apocalyptic edge, they also laid the groundwork for a more historically conscious reading which took seriously Matthew's Jewish roots, narrative structure, and theological intent.

Twentieth-Century Theological Renewal

The crises of the twentieth century which included two world wars, the collapse of liberal optimism, and the rediscovery of Scripture within the church also brought a theological reawakening in the interpretation of Matthew. Historical criticism did not disappear, but it was joined and often challenged by theological and existential readings that reclaimed the Gospel's confessional and moral force.

Karl Barth restored the primacy of divine revelation over human religion. For him, Matthew's Jesus is not an ethical exemplar but the incarnate Word whose authority breaks into human history with sovereign grace. Rudolf Bultmann, though operating within historical criticism, redirected interpretation toward existential encounter: what matters is not the historical details of Jesus' life but the call of the kerygma that confronts the hearer in the present.

At the same time, other theologians sought to reassert the unity of faith and ethics. Dietrich Bonhoeffer's *The Cost of Discipleship* (1937) stands as perhaps the most influential twentieth-century reading of Matthew. Grounded in the Sermon on the Mount, Bonhoeffer distinguished between "cheap grace," which excuses disobedience, and "costly grace," which calls the believer to visible discipleship under the cross. For him, Matthew's Gospel embodied the paradox of grace that commands, and command that grants grace.

In the Catholic tradition, the biblical renewal movement culminated in Vatican II's *Dei Verbum*

(1965), which affirmed the full inspiration of Scripture while encouraging critical study within the life of the church. Scholars such as W. D. Davies and Krister Stendahl advanced a new appreciation for Matthew's Jewishness which focused on its continuity with Torah, its vision of covenant fulfillment, and its use of Scripture. This rediscovery not only bridged the gap between exegesis and theology but also opened new possibilities for Jewish–Christian dialogue, where Matthew could be read as both deeply Jewish and distinctively Christian.

Narrative, Literary, and Canonical Approaches

By the late twentieth century, a reaction against fragmentary historical methods produced a renewed focus on Matthew as a coherent literary and theological whole. Narrative critics, led by figures such as Jack Dean Kingsbury, David Garland, and R. T. France, explored the Gospel's structure, plot, and characterization. They high-lighted the dramatic tension between revelation and rejection, the disciples' journey from misunderstanding to mission, and the inclusio of Emmanuel ("God with us") at the beginning (1:23) and the end (28:20).

Literary analysis underscored Matthew's artistry: his use of symmetry, irony, typology, and scriptural allusion. The Gospel was recognized as a carefully constructed theological drama rather than a loose collection of sayings. Simultaneously, canonical interpretation, championed by Brevard Childs and later N. T. Wright, situated Matthew within the overarching story of Scripture, from creation and covenant to Christ and new creation. In this perspective, Matthew's Gospel is not only one narrative among four but a climactic telling of Israel's story which narrates the fulfilling the Law and Prophets while also opening them to all nations.

Global and Contextual Readings
In the closing decades of the twentieth century and into the twenty-first, new voices brought fresh perspectives on Matthew's Gospel that were rooted in diverse cultural and social experiences. Liberation theologians, particularly in Latin America, read Matthew's emphasis on justice and mercy as a manifesto for the poor. The Beatitudes and the judgment of the nations (25:31–46) were interpreted as a call to solidarity and concrete acts of compassion. Feminist theologians, such as Elisabeth Schüssler Fiorenza, foregrounded the women of Matthew's genealogy and resurrection narrative as agents of divine promise and proclamation, challenging patriarchal assumptions within both text and tradition. Postcolonial interpreters reexamined Matthew's rhetoric of authority and mission ("make disciples of all nations") in the light of imperial history, exploring how power and gospel intertwine in contexts of domination and resistance.

Meanwhile, African and Asian theologians developed contextual readings that integrate Matthew's ethical vision with communal and ecological values. Themes such as reconciliation, hospitality, and stewardship resonate with local realities while expanding the Gospel's global horizon. In these settings, Matthew's Jesus continues to speak as Emmanuel, the God who is present amid poverty, struggle, and renewal.

Theological and Ecclesial Renewal

In recent decades, a renewed convergence between academic exegesis and ecclesial reading has emerged. The theological interpretation of Scripture movement invites scholars and churches alike to read Matthew as both historical witness and living Word. Its closing promise, "I am with you always, to the end of the age," has become a hermeneutical key for contemporary faith: the same presence that animated the first disciples sustains interpretation today.

Thus, the modern history of Matthew's interpretation is not merely a story of methodological change but of rediscovered continuity. The Gospel remains a text of revelation and encounter, commanding rigorous study while inviting transformative faith.

Conclusion

The history of Matthew's interpretation is the story of Christian theology itself. Each age has turned to this Gospel to discern anew the meaning of discipleship, authority, and grace. Medieval monks read it as the charter of spiritual ascent; Reformers as the measure of faith and obedience; modern scholars as a literary and theological masterpiece that unites ethics, Christology, and mission.

What endures across these readings is Matthew's capacity to speak to the church's deepest questions: How does divine authority meet human weakness? What does righteousness look like in a world of compromise? And how is Emmanuel made manifest among his people? The enduring vitality of Matthew's Gospel lies in its ability to answer these questions afresh in every generation, summoning both scholars and disciples to hear and obey the Word that does not pass away.

Chapter 19
Matthew in Contemporary Theology and Church Life

The Gospel of Matthew continues to speak with remarkable vitality to the contemporary church. Its rich synthesis of theology, ethics, and mission has made it an enduring resource for Christian reflection in every age. Whereas modern biblical scholarship has often analyzed Matthew historically or literarily, contemporary theology has rediscovered it as a living text that addresses the moral and spiritual challenges of today's world.

Matthew's Gospel has shaped Christian conscience and imagination more than perhaps any other. Its portrait of Jesus as teacher and Emmanuel, its radical ethic of mercy and righteousness, and its closing commission to disciple the nations have each inspired renewed interpretation in an era marked by cultural plurality, economic disparity, and ecological fragility. This chapter examines several key dimensions of that ongoing influence: Matthew's role in ethical debates, the emergence of global readings, its use in worship and formation, and its enduring challenge to the public witness of the church.

Ethical Debates Shaped by Matthew

Matthew's ethical vision continues to serve as a moral compass for Christian communities navigating the complexities of modern life. Its demands are radical yet grounded in divine grace; its call to righteousness resists reduction to either moral legalism or easy relativism. The Gospel's insistence that righteousness must "exceed that of the scribes and Pharisees" (5:20) has been heard in every generation as both judgment and invitation, summoning believers to integrity, mercy, and wholehearted devotion.

Violence, Nonviolence, and Reconciliation

Few Matthean teachings have provoked more reflection than Jesus' command to love enemies (5:44) and to renounce retaliation (5:38–42). In the modern era, these words have inspired both pacifist traditions and nonviolent movements for justice. Figures such as Leo Tolstoy, Mahatma Gandhi, and Martin Luther King Jr. drew upon Matthew's Sermon on the Mount to articulate a vision of moral resistance grounded in truth and love. Within Christian ethics, debates continue over whether Jesus' teaching constitutes an absolute prohibition of violence or a transformative ethic of reconciliation that may include the pursuit of justice.

Catholic social teaching and Protestant pacifism have found common ground in Matthew's portrayal of mercy as the definitive mark of divine sonship (5:9; 7:12). In contexts of political polarization and war, the Gospel's call to forgiveness and peace remains an indispensable corrective to vengeance and despair.

Wealth, Stewardship, and Economic Justice

Matthew's warnings about wealth and anxiety (6:19–34; 19:16–30) challenge modern consumer culture. The Gospel refuses to separate spirituality from economics: "You cannot serve God and wealth" (6:24). Contemporary theologians and ethicists have interpreted these passages as a critique of materialism and as a summons to stewardship and solidarity with the poor.

Liberation theologians, in particular, have emphasized Matthew's vision of the kingdom as a reversal of economic hierarchies. The parables of the vineyard, the talents, and the judgment of the nations have been reimagined as parables of justice, exposing the dangers of greed and complacency. For Western churches wrestling with questions of sustainability, Matthew offers a moral grammar for economic discipleship in which treasure is measured not by possession but by participation in God's generosity.

Inclusion, Gender, and the Margins

Matthew's genealogy, which includes Tamar, Rahab, Ruth, and "the wife of Uriah," signals a Gospel already attuned to boundary-breaking grace. Modern feminist and inclusive theologies have drawn from these texts to argue that God's saving work transcends social, gendered, and ethnic barriers. Jesus' interactions with women, Gentiles, and the marginalized, such as the Canaanite woman (15:21–28) and the women at the tomb (28:1–10), illustrate a discipleship of inclusion that challenges patriarchal and exclusionary structures within the church.

Contemporary discussions about gender equality, ordination, and the inclusion of marginalized persons continue to return to Matthew's ethic of mercy over sacrifice (9:13; 12:7). In the light of these texts, Matthew's community becomes a paradigm for a church defined not by purity boundaries but by faithful responsiveness to God's inclusive righteousness.

Global Interpretations

The global expansion of Christianity in the twentieth and twenty-first centuries has generated a profound renewal in the reading of Matthew. No longer confined to Western categories, interpretation now arises from a plurality of cultural, political, and spiritual contexts. In these diverse settings, Matthew's Gospel has proved uniquely adaptable. Its strong moral vision, emphasis on discipleship, and portrayal of divine presence speak powerfully across cultures.

African Readings

In African biblical studies, Justin S. Ukpong's *Reading the Bible in the African Context* and Gerald West's *The Academy and the Poor* advocate "inculturation hermeneutics," reading texts like the Beatitudes or the parable of the unforgiving servant (18:21–35) in dialogue with contemporary experiences of injustice and forgiveness. The result is a

Matthew read as a narrative of moral renewal that empowers communal healing.

Asian Readings

In Asia, Matthew has been interpreted within interreligious and socio-political frameworks. Choan-Seng Song's *Third-Eye Theology* and Kosuke Koyama's *Water Buffalo Theology* see in Matthew's portrayal of Jesus the compassionate teacher whose authority is rooted in suffering love. Samuel Rayan of India highlights Matthew's mountain scenes as moments of divine revelation where the wisdom of Jesus meets the wisdom traditions of Asia.

Feminist theologians such as Kwok Pui-lan read the Canaanite woman narrative (15:21–28) as a paradigm for postcolonial dialogue, an encounter that destabilizes boundaries between insider and outsider. Asian readings therefore interpret Matthew as a Gospel of transformation and hospitality in multi-religious societies.

Latin American Readings

Latin American theologians have long regarded Matthew as a charter for liberation. Gustavo Gutiérrez, Jon Sobrino, and Leonardo Boff ground their theologies of praxis in Matthew 25:31–46, where judgment depends upon solidarity with "the least of these." The *Comunidades de Base* ("*Base Christian Communities*") frequently use the Sermon on the Mount as a guide for communal reflection and social action.

Carlos Mesters' contextual commentaries and Elsa Tamez's work on justice and inclusion show how Matthew's Gospel nurtures both personal piety and collective resistance. Within this tradition, the figure of Emmanuel symbolizes God's companionship with the poor, and the Beatitudes become a manifesto for peace and structural change.

Matthew in Worship and Spiritual Formation

Throughout the global church, Matthew remains a cornerstone of liturgy, preaching, and catechesis. Its rhythms of teaching and narrative lend themselves to both proclamation and instruction.

Liturgy and Preaching

Matthew's Gospel dominates the lectionary cycles of many Christian traditions, especially in the liturgical year A of the Revised Common Lectionary. Its parables, miracles, and sermons shape the preaching calendar, offering a comprehensive portrait of Jesus' ministry and moral teaching. The Sermon on the Mount provides an inexhaustible source for homiletic reflection, while the passion narrative anchors the journey from Lent to Easter.

In both Catholic and Protestant traditions, Matthew's texts frame the sacramental life of the church. The baptismal formula (28:19) and the Eucharistic words of institution (26:26–29) are central to liturgical practice. The Lord's Prayer, in its Matthean form, structures Christian devotion across denominations and centuries.

Catechesis and Spiritual Formation

Matthew's Gospel also undergirds Christian education and discipleship. Its emphasis on obedience, mercy, and forgiveness provides a framework for moral formation. Contemporary catechetical programs often draw on Matthew's parables to teach virtue ethics and discernment. The Beatitudes serve as a curriculum for holiness, a pedagogy of grace that forms character rather than merely transmitting doctrine.

In monastic and lay spirituality alike, Matthew's Jesus remains the archetype of the wise and compassionate teacher. The call to "learn from me, for I am gentle and humble in heart" (11:29) continues to define Christian spirituality as a lifelong apprenticeship to Christ.

Matthew in Popular Culture

Matthew's Gospel has also entered the cultural imagination through film, literature, and music. From Pier Paolo Pasolini's *The Gospel According to St. Matthew* (1964) to modern dramatizations and digital media, artists have found in Matthew's Jesus a figure of both authority and tenderness. Its ethical idealism and narrative coherence make it one of the most accessible and evocative of the canonical Gospels. In this way, Matthew continues to mediate between Scripture and the broader culture, inviting new audiences to encounter its message.

Matthew and the Public Witness of the Church

Beyond personal and liturgical piety, Matthew's Gospel continues to shape the church's engagement with the public sphere. Its vision of the kingdom of heaven as both present and coming challenges Christians to live as agents of transformation in society.

The Great Commission (28:18–20) provides the foundation for global mission, yet contemporary theologians increasingly interpret mission not only as conversion but as participation in God's redemptive work for all creation. Matthew's emphasis on mercy, justice, and truth calls the church to embody an alternative social order grounded in love of God and neighbor.

In the modern context of secularization, political division, and ecological crisis, Matthew's Gospel offers a theology of public discipleship. Its call to righteousness is not confined to the private realm but extends to systems of power and care for the earth. The church's credibility, as Matthew repeatedly suggests, depends upon integrity between word and deed: "Let your light shine before others, so that they may see your good works and give glory to your Father in heaven" (5:16).

Conclusion

The Gospel of Matthew continues to sustain theological reflection and ecclesial life in the twenty-first century. Its moral seriousness and theological depth invite the church to faithfulness amid cultural change, its Christology centers discipleship on divine presence, and its vision of the kingdom offers both hope and challenge.

Whether read in monasteries or market-places, in pulpits or protest movements, Matthew speaks with enduring clarity: righteousness is not an abstraction but a way of life formed by grace. The Gospel's Jesus, teacher, healer, and Emmanuel, remains the living Lord who commissions his followers to embody God's kingdom in word and deed until the end of the age.

Chapter 20
Suggested Reading

The study of Matthew's Gospel remains one of the most dynamic areas of New Testament scholarship. Over the past century, new methods and global perspectives have reshaped the field, moving beyond purely historical approaches to include literary, narrative, sociological, and theological readings. This chapter offers a selective guide to major commentaries, monographs, and journal articles that represent the breadth and vitality of contemporary Matthean research.

The goal is not exhaustive coverage but orientation so as to help students and scholars identify essential resources for study, exegesis, and teaching. These works include both classic contributions that continue to shape the discipline and recent publications that broaden interpretive horizons through diverse cultural and methodological lenses.

Bibliography of Major Commentaries and Monographs
Foundational Scholarly Commentaries
France, R. T. *The Gospel of Matthew*. NICNT. Grand Rapids: Eerdmans, 2007.

Davies, W. D., and Dale C. Allison Jr. *A Critical and Exegetical Commentary on the Gospel According to Saint Matthew*. 3 vols. ICC. Edinburgh: T. & T. Clark, 1988–1997).

Hagner, Donald A. *Matthew*. 2 vols. WBC, vol. 33. Dallas: Word, 1993–1995.

Luz, Ulrich. *Matthew: A Commentary*. Trans. by Jerome E. Crouch. 3 vols. Hermeneia. Philadelphia: Fortress Press, 2001-2007.

Schweizer, Eduard. *The Good News According to Matthew*. Trans. by David E. Green. Atlanta: John Knox Press, 1975.

Recent and Diverse Contributions

Brown, Jeannine K., and Kyle Roberts. *Matthew*. Two Horizons New Testament Commentary. Grand Rapids: Eerdmans, 2015.

Carter, Warren. *Matthew and Empire: Initial Explorations*. Harrisburg, PA: Trinity Press International, 2001.

Culpepper, R. Alan. *Matthew: A Commentary*. New Testament Library. Louisville, KY: Westminster John Knox, 2021.

De La Torre, Miguel A. *Reading the Bible from the Margins*. Maryknoll, NY: Orbis Books, 2002.

González, Justo L. *Faith and Wealth: A History of Early Christian Ideas on the Origin, Significance, and Use of Money*. San Francisco: Harper & Row, 1990.

Gurtner, Daniel M., Joel Willitts and Richard A. Burridge, eds. *Jesus, Matthew's Gospel, and Early Christianity: Studies in Memory of Graham N. Stanton*. London: T. & T. Clark, 2011.

Powell, Mark Allan. *Matthew: An Interpretation Bible Commentary*. Interpretation. Louisville, KY: Westminster John Knox, 2023.

Pui-lan, Kwok. *Postcolonial Imagination and Feminist Theology*. Louisville, KY: Westminster John Knox, 2005.

Select Monographs and Journal Articles

Carter, Warren. *Matthew and the Margins: A Socio-Political Reading*. JSNTSup, no. 204. Sheffield: Sheffield Academic Press, 2000.

Hays, Richard B. *Echoes of Scripture in the Gospels*. Waco, TX: Baylor, 2016.

Lee, Dorothy A. "The Faith of the Canaanite Woman (Mt. 15:21-28): Narrative, Theology, Ministry." *Journal of Anglican Studies* 13 (2014): 12–29.

Pennington, Jonathan T. *Heaven and Earth in the Gospel of Matthew*. Grand Rapids, MI: Baker Academic, 2009.

Stanton, Graham. "The Communities of Matthew." *Interpretation* 46 (1992): 379-391.

Stendahl, Krister. *The School of St. Matthew and Its Use of the Old Testament*, rev. ed. Philadelphia: Fortress Press, 1968.

Conclusion

The scholarship on Matthew continues to grow in richness and diversity. From the redaction-critical foundations of Davies, Allison, and Luz to the literary, postcolonial, and global readings of recent decades, the Gospel remains a fertile ground for theological imagination and ethical reflection.

These works together reveal a living conversation that extends across continents and generations. They remind interpreters that every reading of Matthew is both local and global as well as shaped by the Spirit's ongoing work of interpretation. The task for contemporary scholarship is to remain attentive to that breadth: to hear Matthew's voice as both ancient and new, authoritative and invitational, always pointing to the abiding promise of Emmanuel, God with us.

www.ingramcontent.com/pod-product-compliance
Lightning Source LLC
LaVergne TN
LVHW021343080426
835508LV00020B/2098